Augustus Franklin

The Pirates' League

Or, the sea-gull

Augustus Franklin

The Pirates' League
Or, the sea-gull

ISBN/EAN: 9783337182632

Printed in Europe, USA, Canada, Australia, Japan

Cover: Foto ©ninafisch / pixelio.de

More available books at **www.hansebooks.com**

ROMANCES FOR THE MILLION

THE PIRATE'S LEAGUE

OR THE SEA GULL.

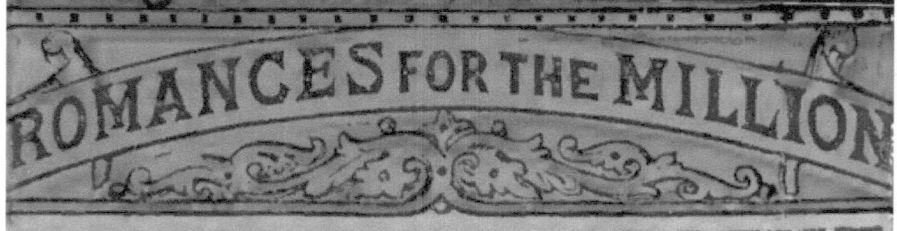

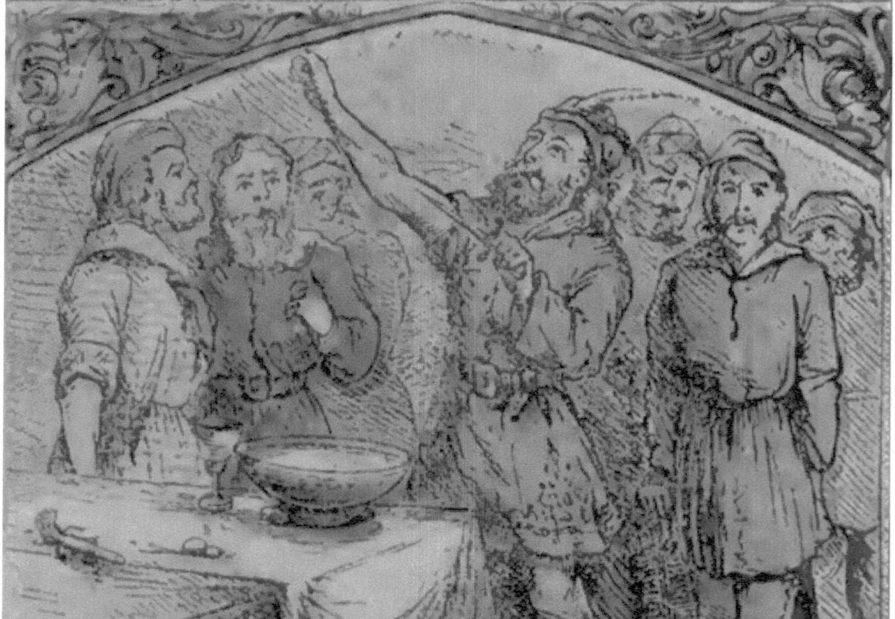

"THEN HIS EYES RAISED TO HEAVEN."

General Publishing Company, 280, Strand.

S. DAVIS & CO.,
Manufacturers,

EVERY DESCRIPTION, 2s. 6d. WEEKLY.
No Extra for Credit.

Complete 55s.　　　15s.　　　Complete 55s.

Illustrated Price Lists, Post Free.

Machines Exchanged.　　Repairs at Either Depôt.

Davis Period Washer, from 20s.　　From 20s.　　Davis Period Bicycle.

Large Sizes, £6 10s.
Small Sizes, £4 10s.

S. DAVIS & CO.'S LONDON BRANCHES:

144, The Grove, Stratford, E., corner of Great Eastern Street.
125, Tottenham Court Road, W., near Euston Road.
67 & 68, Cheapside, E.C., near Bennett's Clock.
10, Hackney Road, E., near Shoreditch Church.
18, Commercial Road, E., near Leman Street.
Period House, Borough, S.E., near St. George's Chnrch.
Wholesale Depot & Chief Office: 15, Blackman St., London, S.E.

S. Davis & Co.'s Sewing Machines, &c., are widely known and Esteemed for their Excellence.

THE PIRATES' LEAGUE;

OR,

THE SEA-GULL.

BY
AUGUSTUS FRANKLIN.

LONDON:
THE GENERAL PUBLISHING COMPANY,
280, STRAND, W.C.

THE PIRATES' LEAGUE;

OR,

THE SEA-GULL.

CHAPTER I.

AMONG the wilds of America, before the forming hand of civilization had constructed to a great degree its works of art and fashioned the boundless wilderness into fields of horticultural beauty—before the wigwam fire had ceased its curling flight among the mighty branches of the spreading forest, and rude barbarianism had concealed itself, in the dying embers of the past, that we would call the attention of our readers.

A few settlers, who had left their homeborn soil, encountered the buffetings of the pitiless storm upon the trackless waste of the ocean, had by their united efforts succeeded in felling the sturdy oaks, and clearing about themselves a spot of ground, sufficient to raise their sustenance, in this northern portion of the western world.

The spring had in its progress approached. Loosening the frost-bound earth from the strong fetters, that in the period of three months, by alternate thaws and repeated storms, winter had forged with its icy hand,

and their almost unyielding durability, began, as the frigid air of heaven diffused itself over the earth in milder and warmer breezes, to flow in liquid torrents down from the mountain heights. This reaction of nature threw life and gaiety on all animate and inanimate objects; and the fields and meadows, divested of their white attire, although barren and frost-bitten, presented a more cheering aspect. Yet, as is often the case, the freezing blasts of the chilly north would frequently return, in the struggling of the milder season to gain the ascendancy over the frigidity of the other, accompanied with its train of attachments, clouds which would intercept the rays of the sun, causing the gloomy effects which followed to be doubly insupportable, and more dreary than before.

After some weeks the contest seemed decided, and more settled weather became the natural consequence, which brought forth the inhabitants of the country upon their husbandry business for the season, and others of the villagers who could well afford the time for sport and pleasure.

It was now at the opening of the month of April, and the vegetable kingdom was issuing out, quickened by the warm showers, from their beds of concealment to beautify and gladden the earth. The merry songsters of the morn and evening had returned from their southern flight, and were fast peopling the groves and filling the air and ear with their notes of rejoicing.

It was an evening in the year 17—, when

the day preceding had been remarkably fine, and the warm influence of the sun, which had set, still lingered in the twilight air, refreshing the senses with an ethereal mildness. In the State of Vermont, upon a road which was in constant use at that time, but now out of service, leading to what has become the metropolis of the State, might, on this evening mentioned, be seen, wending their way at a moderate pace, two travellers, in the persons of a female and a lad about fourteen years old. They evidently had seen better days than their impoverished condition now discovered them, for their garments were, though somewhat worn, of rich materials. The lady was extremely good-looking, and by the resemblance the lad bore her, indicated him to be her son. She was about twenty-five years of age, though perhaps, but for the sorrowful cast upon her countenance, she would have appeared younger. There was something in the appearance of both that at once excited pity and curiosity. They were foreigners no doubt, and perhaps been driven by the reverses of fortune to seek their bread in a distant land. The grief-worn cheek of the young woman gave evidence of this, that many troubles had afflicted her.

As they journeyed along, they frequently stopped to rest themselves, and the frequency of this increased as the day declined and their strength overcome with fatigue by the unevenness of the soil.

They had now in their progress reached a high hill, over which the road, in its course, wended in an angular direction to avoid a too steep ascent. The sun was now hidden from view, which had for the last hour been disappearing rapidly, as they drew nearer to the foot of the hill. Except a faint beam of its light, shot over the brow of the eminence through the opening in the trees made by the road, was visible in the distance. There the travellers stopped and seated themselves upon a fallen oak by the road side, and the mother, who could no longer restrain her strong emotions, buried her face in her hands and wept as she gazed upon her little son, who watched her with the sympathy of one who could feel for another's distress, though he knew not the cause.

After some moments, in which he had painfully listened to his mother's sobs, in the innocence of his young soul said—

"Mother, do not weep, for those tears of thine are as bitter to me as if they fell from my own eyes—can I not relieve you, mother, in some way?"

"No—no—my son," she replied, raising her head, and wiping her swollen eyes, that looked as if they had wept tears of blood. "Poor boy, how little he thinks he is the innocent cause of my troubles," thought she, as she took hold of his arm and drew him nearer to her. "Are you not tired, my dear, this day's walk has been a long one, and I fear too much for thee?"

"No, mother, I think not; I don't care for myself, but rather that you should be weary."

The mother embraced her boy with a countenance beaming with gratification that showed how dearly she loved him. "You can do no more for thy mother, Henry, than to always care for and love her. May heaven reward you for your fidelity, and in its own good time remove the heavy clouds that hang about us."

"I pray that it may," ejaculated the son with delight, that he saw hope beaming in his mother's features, upon which he had gazed with despondency. "We may well be elated with the thought, that the brightest day often succeeds a lowering morning. I am sure heaven cannot be unmindful of us."

At these words their attention was turned to the hill, up which they must ascend before they could reach a lodging for the night, and as the evening was fast advancing, they hurried their steps that they might not be benighted, and they soon gained the summit.

"If we have not misjudged our progress, my son," said the mother, "we shall reach the inn before dark."

"Indeed, we shall, for I can discern it yonder in the opening, not half a-mile distant."

"This is truly charming," she exclaimed, "for I think I could not endure a great while longer this uneven road." Here a thought crossed her mind which caused her countenance to assume a graver aspect, and taking her purse from her pocket examined its contents. "I fear, Henry, we shall not be able to procure a lodging for this small sum for us both," she added.

"We shall have to beg then the charity of the landlord," returned the son.

"I fear it will be a hard one," answered the

mother, who had asked too many times without success for a lodging or a bit of bread, to be consoled by such words.

"Indeed, mother, have hope he may be a feeling landlord, who can sympathise with the distressed; they cannot all be so unfeeling as you say. Come, there is no alternative."

CHAPTER II.

CARLTON DE BLAKE had emigrated from England at an early period, and settled in the State of Vermont—one of the first in the town of Montpelier. He was one of those men whom fortune had blest with an abundance, with regard to physical comforts, and at the time we speak, although at that early age of the country, reputed wealthy. Ill luck often placed him in circumstances where, being innocent, he suffered for the guilty, and but for the abundance of his pecuniary means, would have been an object of pity indeed. In his intercourse with his fellow-men he endeavoured to be strictly honest, but suffered much from the ungratefulness of others, by his promptness and exactness of dealing, who perhaps possessing the very quality he did not, ascribed to him the meagre appellation of Miser de Blake This was exceedingly galling to his patience, but he knew a retaliation would only serve to increase this antipathy, and so contented himself with his title, without ever giving cause for a reverse opinion; but adhering strictly to the Scriptural injunction, "let not thy left hand know what thy right hand doeth," his charitable deeds were his own secrets.

De Blake had a brother some two years younger than himself, to whom was shown, by the parents, much partiality. This unjust proceeding in family government is often the most fatal in consequence; their safety and security is thus placed at hazard, and the utmost disorder and dire animosity takes the place of filial and parental fondness.

Such was the case in the family of de Blake, who lived in a town of Staffordshire, England. Carlton, the present hero of the tale, had never, in the confidence of his father, obtained that credit which he had granted his brother. Indeed the little discrepancies of his youth were not so readily overlooked, but were judged and watched with a suspicious eye.

Thus had the lads grown up to manhood, and the feelings that pervaded each may easily be conjectured.

It was a fine afternoon in the month of September, when Carlton, by himself, had donned his hunting accoutrements and sauntered forth upon an excursion. The sun was shining in slanting rays over the landscape, producing in the feelings a sort of restless melancholy or satiety. He walked along leisurely, at times stopping to satisfy himself as to a rustling he fancied he heard, then quickening his pace to pass a clump of trees, to catch sight of a hawk which he fancied he saw glide behind them. He was so often disappointed that at last he sat down upon a fallen rock to rest himself.

"The old man's grounds are getting rather lean of game," he said, "and like my patience, is rather the worse for scouring. As for enduring this continual toil any longer, I will not—but where shall I go? If I leave before the old man dies, not a cent will be mine—but I am not sure should I remain—perhaps something may turn up in my favour. I may, it is possible, win the old man's favour, for I cannot conceive, and I mean to tell him so, why he should harbour such feelings towards me. If I fail in this, why so be it; Ellen, I know, loves me—how do I know that?—I don't—"

Here the sound of his dog Tracer in pursuit of game aroused him. The noise was at a distance, but he could easily distinguish that it was approaching, and he sprang into a clump of bushes, which afforded him a place of concealment, and awaited the issue.

As the noise of the pursuit grew louder and more distinct, he drew himself up into attitude of firing, in order, when the game passed a little opening in the trees to which he bent his gaze, to lose no time in preparation.

At length he could hear the quick breathing of the pursued, and the quick and eager pantings of the ferocious dog. A dark shadow passed the opening—he fired—a horrible scream rent the air, and thrilled through his very soul. He stood for a moment aghast—cold drops of perspiration stood upon his brow; then, throwing his hands to heaven in agony, exclaimed:

"Good God! what have I done?" and rushed to the spot, where his fears were confirmed of the mischief he had done, by beholding his brother stretched upon the ground apparently dead. "Killed my brother!" exclaimed the heart-stricken Carlton, his own breath almost leaving him as he looked upon the pale features of his dying brother, murdered, it seemed, by his own hand.

"Oh! Father of mercies, why hast Thou afflicted me thus? Oh! this is unsupportable—brother, dear brother, you are not dead—can't be—he does not move, his pulse has stopped—my peace is blasted for ever—a murderer—how can I be myself again—how meet my father—how hope for Ellen—"

"Ellen!" exclaimed William, recovering, "cruel, cruel brother!"

"What!" exclaimed Carlton, astonished beyond all possible endurance. The truth of his critical situation rushed in a moment upon his soul in its fearful and stern reality, from which there was no possibility of escaping. "Brother, do you think me—"

"Cruel, cruel—"

"Have I deserved this—why, wherefore?"

"Do you not love Ellen Stanwood? Ah! revengeful—cruel—" He could not finish what he would say, but fell back to the ground, from which he had partially risen, senseless.

Carlton knew that expostulation would be useless, for all the assurances he might urge in favour of his innocence would be in vain. He knew his conduct towards William had not been what it should have been. This was a very unfavourable symptom; and that he would be considered, even by his father, a wilful murderer; that he had committed the crime in order that he might revenge himself on his brother, now that he had ascertained Carlton loved her, would be the natural conjecture drawn from these several conclusions.

Carlton saw it in this light, and becoming terrified in view of it, did the worst thing possible, which served to confirm his supposed guilty motives—he ran away, and was never afterwards heard of in England.

William de Blake was conveyed by his friends, who sought him, to his chamber, and the best faculty employed to aid his recovery. The extent of his injury could not be determined, and the physicians who attended him could not well hasten his convalescence, consequently many months passed before he was able to leave his bed.

"Ellen Stanwood was the daughter of George Stanwood, the overseer of the estate, and chief counsellor of Baron de Blake, the father of William and Carlton. She was equal in intellectual attainments, if not in birth, to the Baron's sons. Her knowledge of history was immense. She could relate with wonderful precision many, if not all, the incidents recorded in the history of her own country and others.

Her classical knowledge was of no inferior order; for she could read Homer and Virgil in their original, with the exactness of one long studied in the dead languages. To these accomplishments was added beauty of features and symmetry of form, combined with a most winning and fascinating deportment. In person she was of the medium stature, and at this time about seventeen years of age. Mild in disposition, and gentle in conduct, she was beloved by all who knew her. She bestowed her smiles on all without reserve, or apparent preference for the attention of any.

Nor, indeed, as yet, had any dared to approach beyond the common civilities of good breeding. It was not long before she was assailed by the declaration of William de Blake that he loved her.

So sudden, and as she thought, out of character, was this, that she dared not credit the young man with truth. What love could the son of a baron bear to a young girl of her standing—a menial in his father's service? It could not be but that his motives were treacherous, and he had evil designs at heart.

"Miss Stanwood, hope, does not doubt my veracity in making this declaration," said William, after a pause, in which he had noted, in the features of Ellen, wonder and astonishment, blended with confusion and struggling emotions, whether to doubt or believe what she had heard.

"Indeed, sir, I feel much perplexed how to receive this testimony of what I should have deemed impossible to have occurred. Coming from such a source of high rank, a menial like myself can in no wise judge of a superior."

"Madam, you have truly reasons to doubt. But I had hoped—" he added, but he had stopped, for what he would advance he knew would be chiding what was most commendable in her nature.

"I understand what you would say," replied Ellen, "but I cannot but think you could make a choice among these of your own rank more suitable of filling the high station you would offer me."

"I have not the least fear," replied William, "but that the accomplished Miss Stanwood is fitted to occupy any station, however exalted. Indeed," he added, "you now underrate yourself. The son of the Baron de Blake cannot hope to obtain one more worthy."

"Do not flatter me, my lord, for, unused as I am, I may take more readily what you have expressed to be the idle words of a fickle tongue."

"Do not mock me, madam; my sincerity must command better respect. If in me you can find a suitor and a lover, in the true object of his heart, I would be most happy in offering to you my hand."

"To be candid with you, sir, as I should have been at first, I would say in answer, I have no power to form such an alliance as you propose to me. If my will were my own, I at least might give encouragement by promising to consider the matter."

This reply at once put to flight all his hopes—he felt so abashed at this that he confusedly left her presence.

Carlton had never made any protestations of his love to the fair Ellen, but deferred it to a more remote period, as his diffidence prompted him most strongly; he chose rather to live in hope, upon her sweet smiles; for he had not the least idea his brother or any one else had sued to her, in which case he probably would have been impelled to quicken his tardy progress in her affections.

The baron, believing his son guilty of the act of wilful murder, strengthened by his former prejudices against him, could, notwithstanding, now that he was placed beyond a hope of recovery, feel that his treatment towards him had been unjust; and endeavoured at times, notwithstanding that his own conscience should suffer entirely for the whole cause of the bloody deed, smother the conviction that, had management in his family government been what it should have been, such a thing would not have occurred.

But as often as he attempted to banish this idea from his mind, so often by his reasoning to the contrary, would conviction strike more fixedly in his heart that his son had been ruined by his own imprudence. Nor did the recovery of William serve to restore what his fears for him had created, which apparently seemed the chief object of his sorrow—a decline of health. But the repentant father was filled with remorse, and being somewhat advanced in life. soon sank under this heavy burden.

William, now the only heir to his father's property, took upon himself the arduous duty of managing the affairs of the estate; and lived in all the extravagance of his luxury.

He once more went to the fair Ellen for her hand; but it was done with far different motives than his former solicitation. He felt in his exalted station far above her, and wished to chastise her for her blunt refusal when he wooed her in the honesty and simplicity of his soul. Rank and station had made a proud and arbitrary man of him, and he looked down upon his inferiors with disdain. Having the means, he denied himself nothing, and spared not his shining gold for the gratification of his sensual desires. In such a state of human depravity he approached the lovely Miss Stanwood, and with his deceptive arts robbed her of all that made life happy—her virtue.

In due time William was reduced to abject poverty, and to escape from contumely was obliged to fly from his country.

Ellen, who had been secreted for several months by William, with the anxious expectancy of his marriage vows, not receiving that visit from him that she was wont, was soon turned with her helpless babe, by her unfeeling landlady, upon the cold charities of the world.

With a heart dropping under her heavy affliction she wended her way towards London, where she was employed in a family who, pitying her unfortunate condition, rendered her all the assistance in their power.

But, as is often the case when misery has wrapped up the soul and divested us of every comfort that fortune attracted, and in its weight tends to sink us lower and lower, Ellen had been scarcely a week in her new station, and began to throw off her anxiety, when an unexpected incident occurred, which again deprived her of a shelter and a home.

Several articles of value had been missed, and through the treachery of one of the servants they were demanded of the unfortunate; she protested her innocence, but in vain—the theft was charged her—and she had no evidence of her innocence. In this dilemma she was taken before the justice and examined—several spoons were found secreted in the folds of her dress. She was tried and convicted; but was finally pardoned through the intervention of Mr Fitzgerald, who laid before the court her unfortunate condition, and the suffering that her helpless infant would endure should the law have its course, and at the same time manifested his willingness to pay any bond that the court might specify, as a remuneration for her liberty. This was granted, and Miss Stanwood liberated. She afterwards expressing her desire to leave the country, a passage was obtained by the above-named gentleman and, together with a company of emigrants, sailed for the new world.

Mr Fitzgerald was the man in whose family Miss Stanwood had lived, and from whom the articles were stolen; and had he been home at the time of the theft, would have sifted the matter without legal measures, as he afterwards did, though some months elapsed before he made the discovery, and found the servant, who had charged the unfortunate Ellen with the crime, guilty. He afterwards suffered as the law directed, with death.

He confessed before execution that he had placed the articles in the lady's dress.

CHAPTER III.

We now pass over the space of fourteen cold years which brings us to the period when our tale opens.

The inn to which our travellers were directed was not a public one as they supposed, but was the private dwelling of Carlton de Blake

As it is still twilight, a description of this beautiful place may with accuracy be given, and perhaps there exists a peculiarity about it at this hour, which it does not bear at any other, for now that the light of the blazing sun has receded from the landscape, which appears dark by its deep hue of green, the white walls of the mansion and its gravelled walks appear more distinctly. The building faces the road, and is situated on the right towards the east, the land about it is even, inclining gradually to the west, until the inclination is lost in the level surface of a meadow spreading itself to a considerable distance, until arrested by the rebounding forest.

All around appears to be arranged in the most perfect order. Here the road for several hundred yards to the north and south assumes a very different appearance, in one respect for beauty, a bank wall is extended along to a considerable distance; the water courses are turned with greater care, and the ditches cleared from every obstacle that might obstruct the passage of water, in which case it would injure the road; the car-ruts have been cautiously filled, and missiles and stones which are often thrown up by the frost and placed there by mischievous schoolboys have been diligently thrown and piled in neat heaps by the roadside. Trees of a young growth are extended along the wall, and clusters appear in various parts of the farm, especially near the house, forming in their appearance groves.

As our travellers approached nearer, they did but stop to admire, notwithstanding their forlorn condition, and indulge a thought, which this pleasing rurality occasioned to their minds.

The milk-maid, as she strolled from her dairy room leisurely to the farm-yard, with her clean, white milk-pail swung upon her arms, had an irresistible charm in it which our travellers could but admire, not so much the home-spun verse.

The termination of each clause, of which, with a peculiar quirk of the organ of speech, to bring a word, which according to the rules of versification should not have been there, in rhythm with a preceding one; as the sweet, clear melody of her voice which echoed in the distant forest loud and long.

Then there was the loud and boisterous vociferations of the farm boy to the cows as he was driving them from the pasture to undergo their nightly operation under the fair hands of the pretty milk-maid; the bleating of the pair of sheep and goats as they sought a shelter under the covert of some projecting rock or tree for the night. The nightingale in his lofty soarings in the dark air, the whip-poorwill's plaintive notes, and the evening songs of the robin redbreast, served to form a strange medley of the most beautiful in nature's collection.

Soon the cows were enclosed in the farm-yard, and Zedy, the boy, began conversing in familiar tones with Dorothy the milk-maid, by whose side he had come and sat.

Now Zedy, or Zed, or Zedediah was a youth of about seventeen years of age; he was tall, and raw-faced, and of a very docile nature. He was, strictly speaking, a regular greenhorn, and ill-luck seemed to delight to play her ditties on him to the no small uncomfort of Zed.

"Dorothy," he said, after some moments' pause.

"Well, Zed," answered the maid.

"Why, if ye only knew, Dorothy—I fear," stammered Zed, "the bears will eat you—oh, oh, oh."

"What do you mean?" exclaimed the surprised milk-maid. "The bears eat me, what do you mean?"

"Yes, when ye are going home to your mother's to-night."

"Ah! that's what you are up to, is it, Zed," answered the girl, with an understanding look, "want to spark me home, do ye?"

"Ye—ye—yes, Dorothy, if ye can have no objections, I can protect ye, you know," and suiting the action to the word, he was going to throw his arms around her, when the witty maid turned her hand slightly, and spouted a well directed jet of milk into the physiognomy of Zed.

"Go away," she exclaimed. "I'll larn ye, you flax head?"

By this unexpected encounter he was half blinded, and in the circumvolutions of his bony arms to brush the liquid from his eyes, the goad which he still retained in his hand, the use of which he had made in driving the cows from the pasture, coming in contact with old brindle's hide, gave her such a fright that in starting suddenly she kicked the milk and maid over upon the ground. Dorothy uttered a pitiful scream and called on Zed to help her, but Zed, who had now sufficiently recovered his sight, stood gazing at our travellers, whom he discovered in a state of almost bewilderment.

Not heeding the cries of poor Dorothy, after some minutes' gazing he advanced towards them, and in the true spirit of his breeding, bluntly asked them, "Who are ye?"

"We are poor travellers who desire a shelter for the night," replied the woman.

"Who resides here?"

"My master," replied Zed, very honestly.

"And who is your master?"

"A man I guess that wouldn't refuse ye a night's lodging, if ye had plenty of money to pay for it," said Zed, eyeing them more mechanically, as if he had seen no one before in all his life.

The woman at last, in hatred of his many questions, demanded of him with earnestness to intercede for them to his master, and Zed slowly withdrew into the house to inquire if they could be accommodated.

CHAPTER IV.

While this odd scene was being enacted out of doors, quite a different one was going on within. Farmer de Blake was seated quietly in his own room when his neighbour Sinford was ushered in. There was something very peculiar and abrupt in his manner.

Sinford was a man of about forty years of age, of medium size, and gentlemanly bearing. He was not a farmer, but a merchant of the village of Montpelier. He had come from England, and had been in the country some fourteen or fifteen years. He, also, was well to live in the world, and had, during his residence in the village, purchased a portion of land of Esquire de Blake, and built himself an elegant mansion thereon, some half a mile from that of the Esquire's.

His business of late years had been entrusted almost entirely to the hands of an efficient clerk, which afforded him much leisure time, almost the entire of which he spent with De Blake.

In this position the neighbours thus far had harmonized exactly, nothing particular had arisen, except their arguments upon creeds, systems, and politics, to cause the slightest irritability between them. But their disputes, although sometimes carried so far as to cause an indifference to respect, and some hard words in their over-excitement happened to drop, they were, on cooler deliberation, all passed over with a hearty shake of the hand in the end.

As Sinford entered, the esquire lifted his eyes

from a large volume which he was perusing, and turned to his visitor.

"I perceive," said he at length, "that I was a little too hasty last evening in asserting the universality of the law of transmission; upon more deliberate consideration, I could perceive some exceptions."

"That there are exceptions, and very plausible ones!" replied the other, "is very evident, and in fact so numerous as hardly to credit a foundation in truth."

"But I do not doubt it altogether," replied De Blake, "for I do conceive an adaption. It is apparent to my mind."

"It is not to mine. A system not plausible in itself should have no credit. I perceive no adaption in the slightest."

"I do!"

"To what?"

"Reproduction—applied to all orders—vegetable and the animal kingdom. The qualities of one thing are reproduced in what originates from its kind."

"That no one can be ignorant of," replied Sinford, rather sneeringly, and not thinking to what conclusion this assent would bring him. "It is evident that a dog would not spring from a horse, or a sheep from another not of its kind, that's plain enough."

"Very plain, indeed, therefore, a natural law applied in one sense will be likely to hold good in another adaption—where the causes are the same, the results must likewise be. Therefore I was, neighbour," added De Blake, more convinced that he had the best side of the question, "our passions and qualities of mind are hereditary, descending to us in proportion as they existed in our parents."

"But the mind and its properties are not to be considered in the same manner as matter?" replied Sinford.

"Exactly the same," replied De Blake; "for upon the brain depends the mind; if the power of my head be like my father's, my mind will be like his, my disposition the same."

"And all your actions and conduct will be a fac simile, I suppose, according to the same law," said Sinford, triumphantly.

"Neighbour Sinford," said the other, a little vexed. "You bought some land of me?"

"I did, sir," said the other, with a haughty air, stopping suddenly, and turning short in his pacing the room, while a smile stole over his face, blended with a little anger that his neighbour should speak of it.

And as he thought to remind him of his obligations, by way of retaliation that he had worsted him in his argument.

"Your father bought none of me."

"No."

"Thus you see, circumstances have placed you differently from your father, although you may possess the same disposition you have conducted reversely."

This remark was decisive, although the illustration was simple, and trivial in itself, Sinford was abashed, and he sat down, crossed his hands, and looked moodily upon the floor.

"In further illustration of this law," replied

De Blake, determined that he would make his neighbour an entire proselyte, " I have a gift in my secretary presented to me by an Indian, on my first coming into the country for a slight service rendered him, who informed me that it had been given for a service rendered of the same kind in their tribe, from the death of one of their chiefs, a hundred years before."

"But what has that to do with the transmission of the qualities of the mind or passions," said Sinford, gruffly.

"It has much. It may answer to illustrate generally I'll fetch the article, and then we will speak of it more definitely."

De Blake disappeared for a few moments, and soon returned with a short poniard or dagger in his hand.

"There! this is the present," said he, holding it up before the eyes of his neighbour. "The story of this is a very horrid one indeed, and heaven grant that the predictions of the Indian chief as to the office it would perform in time, may never occur."

"What did he know about it?" asked Sinford, taking the dagger in his hand and examining it.

"It's possible that he knew nothing, but it shows how that quality of superstition pervaded the whole of his tribe, through the long lapse of time that has intervened, though none existed when it was presented to me, that lived in the time of the chief, but still the presentiment pervaded as strong in the minds of his descendants."

"What was the prediction."

"The story is brief, and may be told in a few words," remarked De Blake. "The chief of the tribe of Ahuneynas was a very powerful and valiant warrior, with his tribe inhabiting the forest about Boston.

"Manhattan was the most ductily sensitive in disposition and feeling, which distinguished him greatly from other chiefs, or any of his tribe. During his day the white man made his appearance upon this New England soil, and planted his foot as an indisputable right upon the hunting grounds of Manhattan, to which the Indian chief was of a necessity obliged to make a compromise with the white man, and relinquished his right of possession, with a desire to settle himself with his tribes in the thicker and denser forest.

"But the Indian many times came back to express his feelings of sorrow, and give vent to a flow of misgivings, at the fate which had obliged him thus to part with his lands. The high towering altar which at the early dawn of every day he had been taught to stand from his childhood and address his Manito, was the spot which clung most tightly round his heart.

"Near this place lived a white settler with whom the chief became very intimate. The man, who was a father, had an only daughter, her name was Elvira, she seemed an object of marked attention to the Indian, and he was often seen leading her about from place to place with the interest of one who felt a strong and ardent attachment.

"This at first was not noticed, or, if it was, thought nothing of. But when, too late, the father learned that the daughter and the Indian were in love, by the chief demanding of him her hand in marriage. The father was confounded. He knew not what to say, so overcome and surprised was he. His answer at last was a positive denial of its taking place, and ordered him from his house. He obeyed apparently with willingness, and departed.

"Manhattan, however, was not to be refused, and he accordingly watched his opportunity determined to carry off his fair protege.

"The father had remonstrated with his daughter to no purpose. He found her inflexible. He feared what would happen. And rather than she should flee to the Indian's 'sooty guardianship,' see her dead. He watched with vigilance, determined to defeat all plans that might have been made between them for a meeting or elopement.

"At last the former took place, and the latter attempted, when the father, who had at last become enraged, struck his daughter to the earth by a blow intended for the Indian, who escaped.

"The dagger which put an end to his hopes, he found some months after, when he again secretly watched the spot. In the true spirit of the Indian character, he would have retaliated and sought revenge ; but to the father of Elvira the Indian owed many obligations which he could not forget. Besides he knew that in justice, according to his rude sense of right and wrong, he had not been injured, for in completing his desires he would have injured the parent, and the parent, in his impetuosity to seek revenge on him, had more injured himself.

"However foreign this reasoning may appear to an Indian mind, it is perfectly obvious from the conduct of Manhattan that it remained not for him to seek revenge in this present instance.

"He wore the dagger near his heart until his death, as I said before, and gave it to his nearest kin, saying that he had communed with the spirit of the place where the deed had been committed, and learned that the weapon should be held among the tribe till some succeeding years, as an emblem of what would be committed in the future by its kin—the full revenge of their chief's wrongs, if it were observed to be always given, in case of favours rendered, to cancel those of the unfortunate maid's father, which restrained the chiefs from his hostile purpose. When the time should be known, and the favour rendered, it would be presented to a white man."

"Why have you received it?" exclaimed Sinford, who had been listening with attention, his little eyes starting from his head. "Do you not fear that this prediction will be fulfilled upon you?"

"Had I any such fear I would not have taken it, or listened to the Indian with such laughing attention, to so rude, and to me, very incredible story; but out of mere curiosity I have preserved it for the story's sake. Do you not perceive in this the principle I would convince you, that the same passions may be transferred in like proportion, as they exist in the parent, to the disposition of the child?"

"A partial view I have of it," returned Sinford.

"Here is a passage in the Scriptures, which bears a considerable weight," returned De Blake, "which I happened to spy when you came in :

"'And the sins of the father shall visit the children unto the third and fourth generation.'"

Sinford sat silent either from consent to the argument, or that his mind was occupied with other subjects.

Some moments passed and not a word was uttered by either ; De Blake turned his attention to the book he had relinquished, while Sinford sat with his eyes bent upon the floor, now and then raising them and turning his head to his neighbour, and reversing the position of his legs which were crossed, as if to address him, would again resume his former position, as though his resolution was not sufficiently formed, and a few moments more would pass in silence.

At last he broke silence.

"Neighbour !"

"Well ?"

"I bought some land of you," answered Sinford with a self-important air, feeling the extent of the subject he was going to introduce.

"Yes," replied De Blake, recollecting that it was his neighbour's turn to retaliate upon him. A slight flush of shame suffused his features as he thought that his previous mention of the fact had been construed by his neighbour to a wrong meaning. "You are satisfied, I hope," he added.

"No, I am not."

"What!" said De Blake, starting at this unexpected announcement.

"Not satisfied," reiterated Sinford, "nor shall I be till my possession shall extend to the obligation of my deed."

"And do you not possess to its full limits?"

"No, sir."

"What does it specify?"

"It specifies—it specifies—," said Sinford, taking the instrument from his pocket, "it specifies that I am entitled to *all* the land extending to the forest, which comprises the meadow."

"The meadow!" exclaimed De Blake, catching the paper from the other's hand, "let me see!"

"It is plain, very, very plain."

"Do you intend to claim it?"

"Most positively."

"But this is a mistake," said De Blake, a little vexed. "The bargain excluded this strictly and emphatically."

"The deed says *all*—ALL the land."

"Neighbour, why is this? this must be rectified."

"It can't be done," returned Sinford.

"It can—it shall be!" exclaimed De Blake, vehemently.

"It shall not be," returned the other in a similar tone; "give me the paper."

"Not till it is corrected."

"Give me the paper," and Sinford, watching his opportunity, snatched it from the other's hand, upon which De Blake unguardedly thrust his hand into the face of Sinford, whose anger rose to its highest pitch at this bold insult. He raised the dagger which lay upon the table, and rushed towards De Blake, and would have struck it to his heart, but at that moment the door opened, and Zed injected his flaxen head into the room.

At this interruption Sinford suddenly released his hold of the Esquire, while his hand, which was upraised. fell harmless by his side. Confused, he walked to the farther end of the room, while De Blake, recovering himself as much as possible, quelled the rising curiosity of Zed to know what they meant by assuring him that it was all in jest.

"What is your business, Zed?" asked the Esquire.

"Two persons want a night's lodging," said he.

"Who are they?"

"One's a woman and the other's a boy," said Zed, swinging the door open, which gave the travellers at the door an opportunity to scan the room and those within, by a light which hung in the passage-way near the door, a view of the applicants.

Presently a faint scream was heard, and the female fell fainting upon the floor.

Zed, half frightened. dodged into the room, and concealed himself behind the door, trembling with fear, while De Blake approached the lady to lend her his assistance.

Nothing could exceed the piteous cries of poor Henry to see his mother thus insensible.

' Oh! mother, what is the matter?" he said,

endeavouring to support her head from the floor. "Is she dead, sir?" he again added to De Blake.

"No, my son, only fainted; she shall soon be restored."

By this time the females of the house arrived at the door.

"Father, what's the matter, what has happened?" exclaimed Ella De Blake.

"Nothing, my child."

"But something has happened, for I heard a dreadful scream."

"Oh, mercy," cried Mrs De Blake, "the poor woman is dead."

"Do something for my mother," exclaimed Henry, at hearing the announcement.

"Poor little boy, is it your mother?" said Ella, expressing a good deal of pity for him.

"Husband, take the body into the house," said Mrs De Blake, "away from the night air."

"Come in, little boy," said Ella, "father will take care of your poor mother," and she took him by the hand and led him into a snug little room—the one which she and her mother occupied.

"Zed, Zed," called De Blake, "where are you, come and assist me."

Zed at this call obeyed, and soon the fainting lady was taken into the house and laid upon a bed.

CHAPTER V.

In a short time the lady recovered. But she was not herself. Her brain was turned, and her eyes stared wildly; her questions were incoherent expressions, void of meaning, yet having enough to show that her mind had a secret which it had been overpowered with. After an hour or so she fell into a quiet slumber, and it was thought when she awoke she would recover her consciousness.

All the family had now retired except Henry, who sat by his mother's bedside watching her with eager attention, and De Blake, who sat in his own room to attend to any call during the night, if his services should be necessary, as he had some fears the poor woman might be worse, and need a physician.

"There is something in the transaction of to-night which really make me uneasy—the poor woman fainting—but that's nothing but the effects of fatigue—the expressions she made use of when she partially recovered—well, that's not to be wondered at; I have often seen such cases before—the brain being heated by being in the sun—but I've seen that face before, it looks very familiar. I'll creep up to the bed-room again under pretence of supposing I heard a call."

He ascended softly the stairs, and opened the door of the room without noise. Henry had fallen asleep, overpowered with fatigue and watching, the lamp burned dimly upon the stand, throwing a faint light around the room.

De Blake approached softly the side of the bed, and held the light near the head of the sleeper.

"It is a beautiful face," he thought to himself, "who can she be?" He looked again; he saw that sorrow had marked it with its defacing hand. "What a pity one so young as she must die. I have seen that face before," he added still to himself, and he looked again. "Ellen! No, no—and yet it does look like her. It is her—those soft eyelashes—I cannot mistake—Oh! Ellen!" and he involuntarily pressed his lips upon hers. "Ah! poor girl, how came you here? Some cruel person has driven you from your home—I did love thee first, and thou shalt have my pity and protection."

She moved, and he darted cautiously out of the room, and seated himself again in his own.

It may seem strange that the affray should take such a turn between the Esquire and Sinford, when Zed interrupted them, if their feelings are not properly known. Sinford's confusion may be readily perceived to arise from a second thought, occasioned by Zed's entrance, of what he was doing, and a fear that the Esquire would tax him with an attempt upon his life. And De Blake, feeling his critical situation to Sinford in regard to his land, thought that if the affair was passed over, in their cooler moments the fault of the deed might be amicably settled.

As De Blake sat musing upon these things, and upon others that had occurred in his youth, he was startled by a noise overhead, as if some one was entering the house. He paused to listen, and he heard, presently, footsteps receding from the house.

He took the light and rushed upstairs again to ascertain the cause, and in passing the chamber where the travellers were asleep, entered and found the lady gone, and the boy still asleep. What could this mean? She must have arisen in her frenzy, and escaped most cautiously. He resolved to know whither she had fled, and immediately descended the stairs, and proceeded to the field back of the house, and through which she must have taken her course.

He had not proceeded far when he discovered a figure upon the meadow not far off. He quickened his pace and soon came up with it. He was near enough to ascertain that there were two persons—a man carrying what appeared a female under his arm, and making his way towards the forest as fast as possible.

He ventured to hail the figure before him; it suddenly stopped, dropped its burden, and fled to the forest.

The Esquire raised the helpless female from the ground, and found it was the lady he was in search of. Her face was pale, and her eyes glassy, which gleamed most horribly in the silver rays of the moon. He carried her carefully to a fallen pine tree which lay upon the meadow, and inclined her upon it. In doing so he felt something warm trickling down upon his hand, which was clasped around her waist. Upon examination he found that a deep incision had been made in her breast, and a dagger was still sticking in it. But what was his consternation when he drew it out to find that it was the identical one he had had in his possession. The story of the Indian rushed most fearfully to his mind.

Why was it that he should be the victim of

such a fate? Why did circumstances conspire to make him what he was not? A murderer? What could he do?

Filled with sad thoughts and repinings, he sunk exhausted upon the fallen tree, and gave vent to deep grief.

Could man be placed more critically? Could circumstances assume a more conspiring form against innocence, and throw over it the veil of guilt? Esquire De Blake was one of the wealthiest men in the country—he had a liberal heart, though many termed him miserly —his reputation stood high as a man of superior intelligence—a man of piety and truth, whose veracity was unquestioned, and whose excellence respected. Was all these to be overturned, which had been built up with a diligent heart and hand, on a mere suspicion? Was his old age to be shrouded in gloom? De Blake could not but think so.

He ventured to look upon the features of Ellen. He fain would ask her spirit who had done this; what had brought her hither? Could no way be devised to save himself? But those thinking questions fled before the sight of her ghostly form. All the feelings of his youth now rose up that he had cherished for her, then the bitter thought of what had separated them. He turned away and wept. He must be resigned.

Some time passed. All was silent and still. The wind breathed not, but the air rested heavily and listless, echoing but the breathing of the lone living being by the side of the lifeless corpse upon the meadow.

Presently his eye caught sight of a white figure. It gradually advanced towards him. The idea of ghosts at such an hour reminded De Blake that this must be one. He stood aghast. The blood of his heart flowed with a chilly rush through his veins, and then as suddenly back again, leaving a cold perspiration upon his frame, which seemed to freeze him to the spot. The form approached—it was indeed a ghost—it seemed to be that of his brother as he looked when he left him stretched upon the ground, with the blood streaming from his side.

The ghost raised its thin fingers by way of triumph, and grinningly smiled

"But I am innocent," exclaimed De Blake, involuntarily, which brought a grim smile upon the deathly features of the ghost.

"Speak," exclaimed De Blake again, and he stepped forward. "Brother! spirit, what would you with me? If thou hast eyes and watchest the actions of men, thou knowest I deserve not this; wherefore dost thou torment me?" In his eagerness he advanced farther, and fell senseless to the ground.

CHAPTER VI.

Dorothy as usual took her way towards her mother's hut after the duties of the day were done. As it was later than usual for her to go home, her mind was filled with fear, and she frequently stopped to look behind.

For she thought she heard some one stepping upon the under brush and the dry leaves, making a crackling noise.

Thus she passed along, halting now and then, wondering that she felt so fearful, for she had passed the same way a great many times without the least apprehension.

The distance she was to travel was about half a mile before she could reach her mother's habitation, and most of the way lay through the forest. She began to regret at last that she had not consented to Zed's kind offer to accompany her, and resolved at last when she arrived at Noman's hut, an old Indian who had lived for many years there as a hermit, to ask him to accompany her.

There was something of a mystery with regard to this old settler, which had never been solved. He lived alone, and seemed to mind or regard those around him with little or no attention. To De Blake he owed some obligation as he dwelt upon his land, and at times would have some words with him, but to no other except Dorothy and her mother, who often called on him as they passed and repassed his hut, and gave him some little necessaries, would he deign to hold communion.

As he was docile and harmed no one, he was left peaceably alone to enjoy life in his solitude. No one questioned his preference for the place he occupied, or why he did not live with the tribe he belonged, who occupied the country some ten or fifteen miles off.

When Dorothy reached the hut, out of breath, and in a hot perspiration from running, she dashed open the door and precipitated herself into it without ceremony, but to her consternation she found it empty; a fire was burning in the centre, and the smoke was issuing out of the top through the crevices in the roof. Supposing that the old Indian would soon return, she sat down to await for him upon the rude form, or cricket or stool.

She had not been seated long before hearing a tread on the outside of the hut. She arose and went to the door, when the head of a huge bear was projected into the entrance, and the animal uttered a hideous growl and gnashed his large white teeth together, as if he would tear the occupant in pieces.

Dorothy shrieked, and stowed herself away in the furthermost part of the hut, but did not faint or lose her nerves. No, this would not do for a girl like herself born and brought up in the woods; and although she knew her danger to be great, she preserved the utmost command over herself after the first shock of terror. She knew as long as the fire was kept burning the bear would never dare to enter, and thereby kept him at bay by throwing such things as were in the hut to keep the fire blazing.

Zed, after assisting his master to carry the fainting lady to her room, took the earliest opportunity of looking after Dorothy. Zed loved her with all the affection that his heart could boast of, and notwithstanding her indifference to his advances, he still persevered with the diligence of being encouraged in his suit. He often invented means to urge her, by exciting her fears, by telling her the bears would catch her when she went out, to accept of his company. But he had not art enough for the milk maid, who always detected him, and annoyed him perpetually for trying to deceive her.

Zed was a coward, and often manifested the greatest fear on the smallest occasions for it. But still love predominated in the present instance when no danger really presented itself, and he hurried after Dorothy, determined to see her safely home, although she knew it not, as he had often done before.

As he arrived at the hut of the old Indian, he ventured to approach it nearer than his course would lead him, when he heard a dreadful growl and a scream, and as he came round to the side where the entrance was he saw the bear standing at the door, and Dorothy alone within a prisoner. His own dear Dorothy. What could he do—he had no weapon to despatch the bear, and if he was not off in a twinkling his own life would be in danger.

He hesitated, almost a good mind to sacrifice his own life for that of Dorothy's. Now was to be the grand test of his love for her. If he could but kill the bear and release her, she might accept him, aye, love him. He seized a large cudgel which lay near and approached. He made a lunge at the animal, when bruin, turning fiercely round, gave a hideous howl Zed was disarmed, he did not dare another onset, but took refuge in a tree, which he climbed with astonishing agility.

Dorothy ran through the door as soon as the bear's attention was turned to Zed, and fled as fast as her legs would carry her towards her mother's cottage, which she was not long in reaching, leaving poor Zed to manage the bear to his own liking.

Dorothy Antony was the daughter of a poor widow, who subsisted almost entirely upon the charity of her neighbours. Her husband, John Antony, had emigrated to that part of the country about the same time that De Blake settled there; but as fate would have it, he was killed by a falling tree about the time Dorothy was born. So of her father she knew nothing, except what she had heard her mother speak plaintively of him.

Dorothy was a kind and benevolent girl, sixteen years of age, and what is generally termed a fair, buxom, country lass. Her cheeks were red, rosy, and the emblems of health; her teeth were beautiful, her eyes were hazel, and her hair of a sandy hue.

Such, reader, was the girl whom Zed Coby could not resist to love. She was the idol of his heart, and the sweet image that hovered around his bed in the pleasant visions of his slumbers.

He was an odd customer, and Dorothy, although she did not hate, could not make up her mind to love him But still she cared more for him than her actions often indicated.

His birth and parentage were not known, neither could he give any account of himself. He had come to the Esquire's, and he had taken him in, and after a little training, had brought him to become quite serviceable at the farm.

The frequent kicks and knocks he had received from the other labourers at the Esquire's during his first year's apprenticeship never brought forth from him the least inclination to retaliation; but he consoled himself now that he was entering upon his second year, that he should gain from them a share of their good feeling in proportion as he had im-)roved in his duties.

Thus was he placed at the time we have ıtroduced him to the reader, and he was per- ectly content and happy, because he knew not ,hat he could be more so anywhere else.

CHAPTER VII.

Poor Zed. Long he sat in his airy seat, till hour after hour passed away like ages to him.

No relief came yet. Bruin sat watching him intently, having thrown himself upon his haunches; he sat erect, his jetty hair glisten- ing in the moonbeams as it stole through the tops of the trees, while now and then as Zed uttered a loud call, a similar growl escaped the bear alternately.

It was now near midnight, when the old Indian returned. Gladly did the sound of his steps reach the ears of Zed, and delighted he heard the report of his gun upon the air, and he saw the bear fall dead upon the ground. He hurried down from his roost as quick as possible to hank him for his deliverance. He met him at the door of the hut.

"He made you his own."

"Yes, the tarnal critter," answered Zed.

"He treed me slicker 'n an eel."

"What on the airth you got there, Noman?" asked Zed, staring with all the eyes he had in his head.

"No breath 'em, Zed," said the Indian, laying his hand upon his mouth. "No good business in this work."

"How comes it?" asked Zed. "I'll be darned if this aint the very gall that called at our house not four hours ago. And she fainted, and I help tuk up to her room, myself. Aint she got over it yet; what a long faint?"

"No hear. You speak more sober," said the Indian. "She's killed."

"Killed," exclaimed Zed, retreating back with horror at the expression, "who killed her?"

"Me no know, but me guess—no, me no tell you yet."

"Where d'ye find her?"

"On the meadow. Me pass by, saw her, and fetch her here."

"Then ye don't know who done it, ha? tarnation strange," and he cast a suspicious glance upon the Indian. "Didn't I jist heard ye firing yer gun?" asked Zed, supposing for the moment that the bear might have been accidentally shot at the same time without intention.

"No, no, me no kill de white gall. You no tink so?" he said, while a tear stole down his cheek. He fancied now that he might well be suspected, and he felt himself in Zed's power.

"I'll be darned if I don't though," replied Zed.

"No, no, me make you tink more different. Come take her into my hut."

Zed assisted the Indian in taking the unfortunate woman into the hut, and by the light of the fire the Indian examined the incision in the heart, and protested his innocence.

"What are you going to do with the body, Noman?" asked Zed, tremblingly.

"She's no killed yet," said the Indian, looking up with a cheerful countenance, for he observed signs of life in the beating of the pulse and the fluttering motion of the heart.

Zed placed his hand upon the heart, which was bloody, and felt the beating within. "I'll bet a goose she can be saved."

"Me know so," answered the Indian.

"We can take her down to Marm Antony's, where she can be comfortably taken care of," said Zed, a thought coming suddenly into his head.

"But we must keep it secret if she no be well again."

"Certain," said Zed, interpreting the Indian's meanings, "but you will keep her here to-night, for we should frighten 'em out of their wits if we took her there to-night."

"Me keep her safe. You come morrow, then me take her better care. Marm Antony are very kind woman," added the Indian.

"That's no lie," said Zed, "and a tarnation pretty darter she's got too."

"You make her your wife one day," said the Indian, looking up with a smile.

Zed shook his head, and retired towards the door of the hut and looked out preparatory to starting, for he felt no little degree of skittishness, after what had happened to him, in going home. He was once half inclined to stay, but the murdered lady seemed more horrible to witness than his fears of what he might meet in going. So nerving himself at last he started with a run towards the Esquire's, the least noise he heard adding more speed to his steps, while horrid visions flew around as he went, and seemed to follow in his steps.

Zed was just turning around a clump of trees which would bring him in view of the house, when he came in contact with something coming in the opposite direction, which knocked him flat upon the ground. When he sufficiently recovered himself, he looked up— a tall, white figure was standing by his side. He gazed in horror upon the pallid features of the spectre before him.

Presently the ghost spoke in a low and hollow tone which made the blood almost freeze in poor Zed's veins.

"Mortal man, if thou disclose to any human ear anything thou hast seen this night, be assured I'll haunt thee from the grave during the rest of thy life. Swear to me that thou shalt alone be possessor of what thou hast seen. Swear this in the presence of thy God and me, a spectre from the dead."

Zed uttered, "I swear," in a low and trembling tone, and he gazed at the figure as it disappeared, to him it seemed in the air.

He now rose to his feet, and picking up his hat which had been knocked from his head in the collision, he prepared to depart once more, when he observed something upon the ground shining in the dark. He picked it up, and found it was a silver shoe-buckle. This he placed in his pocket, and made the best of his way home, pondering as he went the exceeding adventurous day he had had of it. He was no longer frightened, for fear had become familiar to him, so that he arrived home safe, without meeting anything more adventurous worth mentioning.

The phenomenon of the shoe-buckle Zed could not account for. How it should be lost there he knew not, neither could he conjecture, although he lay awake some time after he had lain himself down to repose. It was new and bright, which showed that it had not remained there for any length of time, and must have been lost there during the day previous. Zed examined it by the light of the candle, and found it of great value. He also discovered upon the back part of it the name of William Sinford. His first thought was immediately to carry it to him, as he knew his neighbour Sinford's name to be William. But then the horrid oath he had made to the ghost, to reveal to no mortal the least that had transpired during that night, made it necessary for him to keep it, so he locked it up in his trunk and kept it safe.

When the morning rose it found Esquire De Blake in his room seated in his chair, under the influence of the most unhappy and painful thoughts. He tried to remember the occurrences of the past night no more, but they crowded upon his imagination in all their vivid reality

The Esquire from this time became a different man from what he used to be. Fear, gloom, and sorrow seemed to characterise his every movement to such a degree that it was observed by the family with some considerable alarm. The mysterious disappearance of the lady created in them many suspicions, which they dared not give breath to. After awhile the dispute between Sinford and himself became known, and to this was attributed the cause of the Esquire's moodiness and extraordinary conduct. A law-suit soon commenced between the two neighbours; at the first term of the court the matter was quibbled to a degree and laid over to the next term. The case was very unfavourable to De Blake, and should Sinford gain the case, the deed had been drawn so wrongly up by carelessness, that not the only small portion of the meadow would he gain, but by far the largest portion of the Esquire's estate.

This seemed indeed damping enough, and were there no other, were enough to drive one mad. So strange an affair seemed to take up all attention, and the mysterious disappearance of the lady was almost forgotten in a few weeks; although a seasonable search was made, yet no traces could be found.

CHAPTER VIII.

ELLA DE BLAKE, of whom we have had occasion to speak on a former occasion, was now at the time our story commences but just in her teens—fourteen years of age. The time when the young creatures, if ever, begin to be beautiful and interesting,—when just emerging into womanhood, to observe the sudden transition from school-girl gaiety to the shyness and modesty of the young maiden,—to mark the womanish gravity detecting the giddiness of youth, which, as if unwilling to leave entirely its young companion, would unconsciously break in to the annoyance of the former, which taken so suddenly for her guardian, the young maiden often, unawares, is drawn away easily into her former lightness, which she had so lately left, as if forgetting but that her gaiety had been laid aside for a day,—at the slightest temptation would renew them.

This was the case with Ella. So extremely sensitive was she of true propriety and correct deportment that the flippancy of her girlhood, which had been as gay as now she would be precise and punctilious, seemed hard to abandon, and often caused many a blush to gather upon her cheek, and many a secret repining, that she succeeded no better in correcting herself or her faults, and as she thought her tardy progress in the accomplishments of a woman.

But she was only detected by herself in these several little discrepancies of her conduct, for none other chided but praised her. Every one was filled with admiration, and the most lavished praise and attention wherever she appeared abroad, seemed attracted as if she had been more than human.

But this applause seemed to have no effect upon the heart of Ella De Blake, or her bearing, which is the means of so often ruining many that are beautiful. She still condemned herself, still lamented that she was no better. Vanity seemed to form no part of her disposition. Her keen perception and discrimination of what was commendable prevented it. Although she was extremely beautiful, she regarded it not with pride, or clothed it with a false air of self-esteem. This perhaps made her more beautiful—for beauty unadorned is the most beautiful. It is as nature formed it, and will be admired wherever it is seen.

Yet Ella could not discover in those mild, blue eyes of *hers* any peculiarity that should distinguish them from those of others, or in the fair outline of her exquisite features, more beauty than she beheld in others. The tresses of her auburn hair she arranged with taste, 'twas true—but still she knew not that they hung more beautifully or gracefully upon her fair white neck than those of her companions, or her form more symmetrical, or the nimbleness of her feet prettier or more bewitching. Indeed, she saw something in them to condemn, and wondered at the praise and flattery that others bestowed upon them.

Ranger Sinford was the son of Sinford, neighbour to De Blake, whom the reader is already acquainted with. To Ella, Ranger had extended the greatest attention from his youth. They were school companions, and it is fair to suppose that an attachment existed between them, as they say love begins when the heart is young and tender, and Ella could not but admire the kindness of Ranger, as he was always sure to wait for her every morning at the door, and return every evening home with her from school. Indeed, she felt grateful, and showed him many marks of affection.

Ranger was of her own age, and very pretty in appearance ; but there was not that worth in him that so often excites admiration even in others. There was something lacking in his composition which could not be made up by any conjectures of the mind, as an equivalent to overlook his faults. Nor was this defect erased by man's accomplishments and the experience of years. He remained the same.

Ella saw this, and, as she grew older, her affection grew less and less, until she thought herself more happy when out of his company. Yet she knew her parents and his delighted in them, and often spoke, as parents often will, of their children ; that is, they seemed to enjoy each other so well now, when they were young, they would naturally love each other when older, and the attachment which was so strong could meet with no result but a union in some after time. She dared not give vent to her own inclinations, but continued as usual, but not to so great an extent, to show him her favours, for she knew if she did, it would be hypocrisy, and therefore extended attention to him in proportion as she had receded from her former feelings by age.

It was not so with Ranger—the reverse from her—age increased what his youth had feebly begun, and as each day brought him in the company of Ella, he saw something in her which caused him to love her more than he did the day previous. In the zeal of his warm passion, he lived on her smiles by day, and on her image dreamed of bliss by night.

Such was the case between the doating son of Sinford and the beautiful daughter of De Blake, when the incident of the first chapter of our tale occurred.

It will be naturally anticipated that Ella would seek, if she could with no discredit to herself, for some one whom she could love better, and whom she could not hold aversion to, and she prayed, although yet young, that the hopes of the parents would not be fulfilled.

From the evening that she saw Henry Sherwood, for he bore his mother's name, all the little affection she bore Ranger took its flight, nor ever after visited the region of her heart.

CHAPTER IX.

THE summer, which we mentioned as approaching, had passed, and with it had fled the gloom which the loss of his mother created upon the mind of Henry Sherwood. Although he felt not now the grief he had first experienced, the occurrence was painted as visibly upon his mind, and never would it be effaced, but would ever linger in his thoughts, to haunt him with continual painful conjecture.

His heart was young, and grief soon dies away, nor leaves a trace that will be so severely felt when long time has advanced, as is felt in more mature age.

The kindness of De Blake had taken the charge of Henry, and gave him a home beneath his own roof.

This was annoying to Ranger, and created a feeling of jealousy within him. Although he never refused his company, he owed him a grudge at heart. This suspicion was not wholly ungrounded, for he noticed many times, when the three were together, that Ella smiled more sweetly upon Henry than upon himself.

Ranger did not retaliate, for he was not sure that Henry solicited her regard, or that she bestowed more upon him than was called for in the extension of the civilities of friendship and respect; yet he feared they were together too often for his own comfort, and resolved to prevent it by gentle means. He would bestow upon him a kindness that, as he was dependent upon charity, he would not refuse, but thank him, without the least suspicion of selfish motives being at the bottom.

He reverted to his father, and requested him to take Henry and place him in his store as a clerk, for the young man did not like to be dependent, without some remuneration, upon the charity of any one.

The father made some objections to his request, and asked some deliberation; but Ranger knew his influence over his father, and did not leave him till he had consented.

This offer was extended to Henry, who considered it very generous in Ranger, and he embraced it with many thanks to him for the kindness and interest he took in his welfare.

"I know not how I shall be able to remunerate you, my kind friend, for thus interceding for me. Indeed, you are kind."

"No, no, my dear fellow, the pleasure I feel in assisting you well compensates me for the trouble. Indeed, it's no trouble; for when a man does good for the pleasure, and not for hire, why, it's no trouble; it's wages of itself, nor needs compensation."

"I am well assured of your generous feelings—that they are governed by the strictest motives of right," replied Henry, "and may you ever prosper in your right worthy purpose. I presume my inexperience may present many difficulties in my new station."

"Never fear for that. I shall be most happy in assisting you further, if occasion calls," he replied in his earnestness, unguardedly emphasizing the word further.

"You are too kind."

"Not so kind but I might be kinder," replied Ranger, as he bade him good-bye and wheeled triumphantly on his heel and retraced his steps toward home.

Henry could not but feel the greatest regard for his friend, and cherished him as a brother ever after.

CHAPTER X.

INSTALLED in his new situation, Henry was deprived of the company of Ella De Blake and Zed, whom he had made his trusty friend. Although he dared not think he loved the Esquire's daughter, he felt now that he was away something in his person he could not define. Did he love her, what! the jewel of another's heart? And to his own friend could he be so ungenerous? He shuddered at the thought, and banished the idea a thousand times from his mind. But still, as his feelings drooped by times, this feverish throbbing made him think of Ella in spite of all his endeavours. Nothing had ever passed between them that caused the slightest evidence that what he felt was founded in truth. Why it was he could not tell. Sometimes he would resolve to leave the place, and in foreign parts forget all he had seen and heard of her. But he would as suddenly fly from the idea, for he recollected he had not means, and then he knew when he reflected that her love by an age he could not erase from his mind, and would be with him present, there as here. If he remained here, he could satisfy an inclination at times of seeing her, which for the while was a temporary relief.

It was one afternoon in the following spring when Harry had gained his eighteenth year, and a year from the time we have introduced him, that he was in the store alone. It was a beautiful afternoon in the month of March. He began as the beauties of the sun began slowly to decline to his western bed—a fit time for romantic thoughts, and love affairs, that he began to think of Ella. He counted the days that had ensued between the time that he had seen her. He found that it had been near three months. Wondering why it had been so long, he began to conjecture a cause. She might be sick—no, that could not be, for Zed would have told him as much, not confidentially, as a matter of news. But he wanted to see her, and see her he would, if he was under the necessity of going personally to the house and call on her. "Ah!" he exclaimed, "there is no use in denying but that I love her. Is there any harm when I cannot help it. I do not rule my own feelings—but 'tis God, who is the author of all love. I'll write to her and learn my fate at once."

And as he spoke he seized a pen and paper, at the writing desk, and commenced—

"DEAR MADAM:

"This bold and intrusive act I hope will be pardoned when you consider that the writer ——"

He read over and over the few words he had written.

"Ranger and Ella both will laugh at me for this. No, I won't write a letter. Perhaps I might write a verse of poetry."

He accordingly commenced as follows:

"I know not why I love thee,
　Or why thou seemest divine,
When reason plainly tells me
　Hope can ne'er be mine.
Yet thy image lingers here,
　Unbidden and unbound,
My power but feebly guards
　The unruly heart around.
In love I'd rival none,
　No, I scorn the beggar name,
Sooner may my heart be stone,
　And never feel its flame."

Scarcely had he finished writing these lines when the fair subject of them entered the store.

Turning to observe who the customer was, he discovered it was Ellen De Blake. A nod of recognition passed between them, which brought a blush to each of their faces. They seemed to be rather confused, especially Henry, who in his earnestness several times found his eyes fastened upon her so steadfastly that he was hardly conscious of the meaning of her question.

"Have you mitts?"

"Yes," replied Henry, taking from the shelf a box and placing it before her on the counter.

"What is the price of these," she asked, putting one of them upon her soft velvet hand.

"Two and threepence," he said, blushing deeply.

Ella then selected a pair, and Henry, after using the precaution, dexterously slipped another in the place of the one he had seen upon her hand, rolled them carefully in a paper, and bidding her good day, she departed.

"Oh, you much honoured little thing," he said to the mitt, pulling it from his pocket after she had gone. "How blest was thy situation upon that fair hand," and he pressed it to his lips again.

"Where is my letter, my poetry that I was writing?" he exclaimed, on going to the desk and finding it gone. "Is it possible that I have taken that sheet of paper in my absence of mind, and used it for wrapping paper. Oh, I had rather given anything in the world than it should have occurred, so badly executed: if the penmanship had been better I would not have cared about it. Indeed, I would not have it seen for worlds. But I can't help it now. She has got it; she will think what she pleases of it, I shall never dare to look her in the face again. I hardly dared to before, much more now."

CHAPTER XI.

ELLA returned, but not as she had done frequently before from the village. Her mind was more than ever filled with the image of Henry. "I cannot mistake that glance, it was intended for me,—what an expression of feeling. Why have we not breathed this to each other. There is something in his mind, and it is intended for me. Oh, how many pains would be spared—how many sighs and tears withheld, could I but know this. Oh, cruel fate, that I am compelled to receive the attentions of a man I do not love. Nay, I almost detest Ranger. Henry no doubt but for him would have hinted his feelings to me long ago."

She had now arrived at her own home. Although it was not far, she had been longer than usual.

She had barely been seated and rested a few moments from the fatigue of her walk when Ranger entered, armed and equipped as a sportsman.

"Ah, Ella, returned," he said on entering, "been to the village I understand. Been purchasing?"

"A few things—a pair of mitts and other little trifles."

"Did you see Henry?"

"I—I--did, I bought my mitts of him."

"Ah! let me see them—see if he has cheated you."

"Cheated me," said Ella with surprise. "He cheat? I should as soon think of you as him."

Ranger felt a little surprised at these words, but a cloud came over his brow. He did not like their import, things reflected too strongly for the interest of Henry. In a calm tone he said, by way of apology,

"I meant nothing, Ella, why should you be offended?"

To him who was jealous, little things had the greatest effect, and they were as soon as seen construed to that one point, that he was being rivaled.

After a few moments conversation farther, in which he detected some other little things that fed the flame of his jealousy, he departed.

As soon as he was gone, Ella took the paper from her pocket, and tremblingly read the lines placed upon it. They were evidently those of Henry's, it was his handwriting. She could scarcely believe what her eyes saw

"How generous he is," she said, "towards Ranger; he would not love me for the sake of rivalship. No, he loves from a purer motive. He knows not why he loves me. Ah! Henry, I know not why I love thee. How hesitatingly he is, how he fears to offend, how he fears to flatter me. This I know he did not intend I should see, or he would have wrote it more plain.

"In his thoughtful moments he has done

this to improve his mind, for it betrays in its execution his perplexity and uneasy condition. Dear Henry, you shall no longer be a stranger to my thoughts. I will relieve you, your mind shall have at least one joyous moment by hearing my declaration, if no more," and she ran to her secretary and took from it pen, ink, and paper, and commenced writing a letter to him ; but she found this task more difficult than she supposed. How she could convey it to him first occurred to her, without suspicion, for she had observed that Ranger watched her narrowly. She at length threw down the pen, as the thought occurred that she had no evidence upon the sheet that Henry meant her ; perhaps it was intended for some other, and resolved to lay the subject by for more deliberate consideration and evidence that might justify her in declaring herself to him.

Ranger was, from this day's observation, well assured that Ella was no longer what she had formerly appeared to him. He saw plainly that Henry was an object of her regard, and notwithstanding the precaution he had used, he perhaps had instilled the honied words into her ears, and gained, over him, her love ; this could not be otherwise to him—from why that paper she unrolled from the mitts, and placed so carefully in her pocket, for fear he should see it. Did not his own eyes read "Dear Madam" upon that portion nearest to his sight ; this was a love letter—he could think no otherwise than that it contained love, a declaration, an entreaty.

Filled with these thoughts he went toward home, plotting on the way how he might rid himself of Henry, or separate him so widely from Ella that he could have no communication with her in any form, either by look, word, or writing.

Ranger's mind was adequate to his purpose, and there was nothing but he dared do to attain his ends. He was what would be vulgarly called a "spoiled child." Therefore he was not long in conjecturing some means of effecting his purpose

CHAPTER XII.

Mr Sinford had liked Henry so well in his capacity, that he entrusted to him in the store many responsibilities.

It was one morning, not many days after the incidents named in the preceding chapter, that as the chief clerk went to make change for a customer, he found there was no money in the drawer. He thought strange of this, as he knew that he had left a quantity of small pieces there the night before. But supposing the possibility of his being mistaken in regard to his leaving any there, let it pass and thought no more of it till he assured himself that there was thieving going on by leaving, intentionally, a quantity of money in different parts of the store to satisfy himself.

Being well assured that some one was thieving he mentioned the circumstance to Sinford, who ordered a watch to be set in order that they might detect the burglar.

Not the least suspicion rested on Henry or any one belonging to the establishment.

Henry, notwithstanding, felt very uneasy that it should have occurred when he was there, for, although he was innocent, being young and but lately put into the store, yet he felt afraid that the crime might be laid to him.

A watch was accordingly set, and for several nights kept up, with the hope of detecting the thief. But he came not—and it was given up at last, surmising that the thief, whoever he was, kept an eye on their movements.

In order to ensure himself of this fact, the clerk resolved to watch privately, unknown to any one in the establishment, for he began to suspect that it was him that he did not wish to suspect—Henry. And in order to relieve himself of such ungenerous feelings towards the young man whom he so dearly loved, hid himself behind the counter, armed for the purpose.

Ranger, whose delighted ears were filled with the reports from the store, lost no time to put his plans into execution, and to terminate them as speedily as possible. Although the clerk supposed himself secreted in the store unknown to any, yet he had not escaped the vigilant eye of Ranger. Now was the time for him to discover to the world the one he wished to, as the villain.

Henry had retired to his bed on this night as usual, thinking no harm, and hoping that no more burglaries would be committed, for he knew that should there be, he would be suspected.

But soothing himself from his fears by the thought that the innocent would be protected by Him who overruleth all things, and offering one prayer for the divine blessing upon the spirit of Ella, he fell into a quiet slumber.

Not long had he enjoyed this sweet repose, when he was awakened by a loud knocking at his chamber door, and upon arising and opening it, he found it to be Ranger.

"Excuse me, Henry, for this late interruption, but I was urged to it by the entreaties of father that I would come to you and ask you if you would go to the store and get his pocket-book, which he left in the desk, accidentally. He fears somewhat for its safety, after what has happened."

"But how am I to get into the store to-night? Mr Riley has got the keys."

"Never mind that, here is the key to the back entrance, which I brought with me lest you should not have the other."

"Very well, I will go immediately," said Henry, unsuspectingly.

"You will bring the pocket book to the house."

"Yes," he said, as he prepared to dress himself, and Ranger departed.

A few moments were spent, and Henry was prepared to execute the supposed commands of his master. Not a thought of his danger, or a supposition that entering the store at this time of night would be critical to his safety should he be seen, till he arrived at the back entrance and placed the key in the door. A thought struck him. He trembled with fear.

How like was this to housebreaking. He withdrew his hand from the door handle and relented, resolving not to enter. But that the property should be safe he would remain all night and watch it.

He contended for some moments with these emotions, and assuring himself once more of no harm as he was not a robber, advanced to the door, turned the key, and opened it. He entered cautiously, and knowing the direction and position of the desk, concluded he would not strike a light.

He groped in the dark, placing his hands in advance of his head lest he should come in contact with whatever might be in his way to the desk, which he found without difficulty. He unlocked it, and opened it, thinking the pocket book would be the first thing in his reach. It was not there. He was filled with fear again that perhaps the thief had been there before him. "Perhaps it may be in one of the drawers," he thought to himself, but which he could not conceive.

A light was now necessary, and he searched round in quest of the tinder box, which he soon found.

The clerk was still beneath the counter, listening tremblingly to the movements of the burglar. He knew not how to proceed, whether to fire at him in the direction he guessed he was, or to strike a light and rush out and secure him.

The former mode he condemned at once, for it was ten chances to one that he should hit him if he fired. To rush out and secure him was hazardous. for the villain might be armed and fire upon him.

So, unprepared, and fearing how to act, he remained until he saw that he had struck a light, and to his astonishment beheld that the person was Henry ; and, when he had advanced toward the desk in search of the pocket book, beneath which he had placed himself, he seized him by the leg and held him fast.

Henry uttered a shriek of terror, and to his astonishment, Riley issued from beneath the counter and stood before him. Neither spoke a word for some time, for the emotions of each were beyond expression, except in their pale countenances and trembling limbs.

"Ah ! then, I have caught you, have I ?" said the clerk in a melancholy tone, eyeing him with pity.

"Mr Riley," exclaimed Henry, looking at his feet, " my motives are honest ! "

"Honest ?" reiterated Riley.

"Ay, and Heaven knows that I am innocent."

"How innocent ?"

"I was sent here."

"By whom ?"

"Ranger."

"Ranger ? "

" Yes : he wished me to come to the store, by the express wish of his father, and secure the pocket book in the desk, as he feared for its safety."

"Ah," said the clerk, taking the light from his hand and going to the desk, "then you see, it is not here," he said, opening each alternately as fast as he could. "Henry, Henry, this is false. I fear you are guilty of a crime that may cost you your life. Come, come with me. I am bound to deliver you over to justice."

Henry fainted and fell senseless to the floor.

CHAPTER XIII.

"Ah! who would have thought it?" said Ranger Sinford, entering the apartment in De Blake's house the next morning, where were seated Ella and the rest of the family.

"What do you mean?" asked Ella with some surprise.

"That Henry would be guilty of theft," said Ranger.

"Henry guilty of theft!" exclaimed they all, starting with astonishment.

"Yes; he was arrested last night in the store by Mr Riley, in the act of taking money from the desk."

"Oh, Heaven support me!" exclaimed Ella, turning as pale as a sheet.

"Did he steal anything?" she asked faintly.

"Not then," said Ranger; "but the clerk has missed money from the store before, and at last resolved to watch and detect the thief, if possible."

"Was he suspected before?" she earnestly inquired.

"No, I believe not."

Henry was carried before Sinford, to whom he related all the circumstances that had occurred the night before; and, before Ranger demanded an affirmative answer to the question,

"Ranger Sinford, I demand of you, in the presence of your God and these gentlemen here, to say that you came to my room and desired me to do that which, had it been true, was no harm; but, being false, has made the doing of it appear like roguery, and involved me in this difficulty."

Ranger blushed a little at this injunction, but assuming a calm and brazen front, denied all knowledge of the proceedings.

Thus stood Henry, a condemned yet innocent youth. All hope was now gone, and he sank down into a chair stupefied.

Ella De Blake had been entreating her father to use all his efforts to save Henry from the fate that awaited him. Accordingly, he repaired to Sinford's house, where his intercession at length procured Henry's release, on condition that he would leave that part of the country.

He hurried to his lodgings rejoicing that he came off so well, and prepared himself for a departure, whither he knew not.

As it was early in the day, he thought he would call on his benefactor and thank him for his kind interference in his behalf.

As he drew near the house, recollections of many things were exciting his bosom. His lone and forlorn condition arose in a full tide and engulfed his soul.

Then there were the many little ties that bind one to a spot on earth, and as he neared the house, he leaned upon the gate by the road-side for support, resolving to go no farther.

He had not remained there long before Zed spied him, who was in the enclosure, and came running towards him with all possible speed.

"Now, Master Henry, this is a tarnation hard job for ye any how."

"Have you nothing to say by the way of encouragement, Zed?" asked Henry, fearing that by his silence he had incurred his distrust.

"None believe you guilty," said Zed, "but those who accuse you. I believe some infernal scheme is going on to injure you. Come, let's go to the house, perhaps you'd like to say good-bye to Ella and the rest of the folks."

"Yes, but do they not believe me guilty?"

"Not a bit, not a bit," said Zed, pulling him by the hand.

Henry reluctantly obeyed, and Zed led him to the house.

After bidding them adieu and thanking the Esquire, Henry took his leave and proceeded, the way he had entered, into the road.

As he was passing through the garden he heard a light step behind him. On turning round he beheld Ella who stopped and looked very much confused.

Who could describe the boundless joy that filled the bosom of Henry. He could well bear now the contumely of a world, knowing that he had the forgiveness and confidence of one who was more than the world to him.

Although the lovers expected never to behold each other again, they unburdened their hearts of a load that had hung gloomily upon them. This was a great relief, and Henry arose, kissed the fair forehead of Ella

De Blake, bade her adieu, and with a light heart wended his way down the road, occasionally turning his eye back to catch another view of the spot where dwelt one whom he loved.

Let us follow Henry to the city of Boston, whether he bent his way.

Henry found employment in a store in Washington Street. The firm of C—— & Co. was the wealthiest that the town could boast.

Here he gained the confidence of his employers, and soon was the head clerk of the establishment. What carried him to this station in so short a time was the manifestation of his fidelity for the interest of his employers.

Henry was a student in his leisure hours, and his habit of much study brought on a desire to become a proficient in learning. He wished a profession. A quiet observance of things and appearances among men had enabled him to judge of his own merits and abilities. He thought he might cultivate to the most advantage and profit his intellectual faculties.

The amount he had now realised presented an opportunity of acquiring an education in a profession, as his primary studies had been gone through, which he thought would be the law. The law in the rising of his useful ambition he saw was the most direct road to public distinction and honour.

Accordingly he made known to his employer, Mr C——, his intentions, who, though sorry to lose him, congratulated him on his resolution, with many assurances that he would be his friend and protector in need.

CHAPTER XIV

FIVE years have passed since our imagination, reader, has been made acquainted with the supposed events mentioned in the first chapter of our story.

Let us now return to that part of Vermont we first saw Henry and his mother wending their solitary ways across the country in quest of a shelter and a home. There is not so much of wildness in the country as it formerly presented—houses appear more thickly, and spots of cleared land around them speak well of emigration.

As we pass again the delightful dwelling of Esquire de Blake, on our way to the village of Montpelier, as our next scene will be there, we discover nothing but disorder and confusion. What is the cause of this hue? The spoiler has been there. For why has negligence taken the supreme rule over everything pertaining to the once beautiful home of Ella De Blake. Where can she be? The once so beautiful, when with her growing womanhood it should have increased to full bloom, the admiration of all.

Yes, gentle reader, she is still beautiful, but the rose has partially faded, her cheek wears but a tint of its former glow. But how came this? Ask her not, for her heart is too full of feeling for her poor father, who has been unfortunate. It is not her own sorrow but his which she suffers—that has robbed her of her bloom. In the village, reader, to which we will go, you will see her. In a small tenement in a low but neat cottage in a by street, lives the once wealthy Esquire de Blake, with his only daughter and child for his companion. By his daily toil he manages to get enough to support himself in a tidy manner. Ella takes the charge of their little apartment, and manages the household affairs with becoming cheerfulness. Her mother is dead, and the only pleasure she now feels is in pleasing her surviving parent, who bears with great fortitude, by his daughter's consolation, the misfortunes of his life.

As we look into the snug little room, we discover the occupants sitting near the window facing each other, looking out at the passers-by. De Blake looks as nearly as possible as he used to, except that a few gray hairs have stole into his dark auburn hair, and care made a visible impression on his countenance. How beautiful Ella looks, although somewhat pale.

"Father, do not sigh at what cannot be helped. Our lot is hard but many have harder ones than we."

"Ah! my child, my dear Ella, I cannot always suppress my emotions, they come so strongly upon my heart that I often give way. Sinford, why should he be so villanous," exclaimed De Blake, warmly; "when I thought the business settled by the compromise for Henry, he still persisted to ruin me in a suit-at-law, founded neither on right or justice. Oh, this is enough to drive one to madness."

The two remained for some moments bathed in tears, their hearts filled with painful emotions. At last De Blake broke silence.

"This Sinford," he added, unwilling to give up the subject, "has incurred a displeasure against me some way or other—heaven only knows how; but this act it is far beyond any human feelings can bear; it is an act that should glut the most brutal revenge—death would not have been half the cruelty."

"I am glad, father, it is no worse. For my part I can consent to 'smile in tears,' if heaven has designed it so, to the day of my death."

It was not many days after the above-mentioned interview between the father and daughter in distress, when the latter was thrown almost into a state of frenzy by the arrest of the former on an indictment of murder.

A great excitement was in the village, and everybody was flocking to the farm and meadow which it was known was once owned by Esquire de Blake. In the meadow, beneath an old fallen pine tree, had been found, on removing it for some purpose by the workmen of Sinford, a human skeleton, and a dagger known by many to have been or in the possession of the esquire. The mysterious disappearance of a lady some years before was now thought to be accounted for; she had been murdered by some one and buried there. The dagger was recognised, and it was probable that it could not have been used by any other but its owner—*i.e.*, no evidence could be had to this effect. The lady was seen at De Blake's house by Sinford, and she had fainted upon her first seeing him, which indicated strongly against him that some difficulty must have occurred between them previously. The lady, it was conjectured by many, had with her the cause of difficulty, and rather than incur the charge she might urge against him, he had put her quietly out of the way.

Ella was seated by her window one or two evenings after the arrest of her father, when she was aroused from her gloomy thoughts by the sound of a well known voice near her, and looking up she discovered it to be Zed. He was so altered that she scarcely knew him. His tidy habit and improved look almost made him an entire stranger. At the sight of him, for he had been absent years, she seemed to forget herself, and appeared to be transported with joy But as soon as he inquired for her father, her grief returned with redoubled force.

"Why, mistress Ella, what has happened?"

"Father has been arrested for murder."

"Murder!" exclaimed Zed, "Oh! horrible! when did it happen?"

"Some years ago, it is said," returned the forlorn girl, resuming her weeping.

"Some years ago!" reiterated Zed, "by Judas I have it," he said quickly. He seized his hat, and placing it upon his head, left the house.

Zed had not proceeded far when he was met by a genteely dressed gentleman whom he did not know.

"Why, Zed, don't you know me," said the stranger.

"No, sir."

"What, not know me?—Henry."

"Yes, yes," said Zed, again scrutinizing him for a moment, and then gripping his hand firmly, he gave it a hearty shake.

"Why, Zed, you seem to have spruced up a little; where have you been—living in the village—left De Blake's?"

"Yes, long ago; poor man! he seems to have been quite unfortunate since I went off into the city to live."

"Unfortunate—how, Zed?"

"Lost his property, and that aint all either."

"What else?" said Henry, eagerly. "Where is Ellen?"

"She lives in that alley down there. She told me just now that her father had been thrown into prison."

"For what?"

"It has been discovered that a lady—no—Henry—" hesitated Zed. "Your mother."

"My mother," exclaimed Henry, with astonishment. "What would you say?" he demanded.

"That it is supposed he murdered her. But she is not dead," continued Zed.

"Does she live, then?" asked Henry, gasping for breath.

"Yes."

"Zed, I will not make myself known to any one yet, but we will proceed to learn the state of affairs concerning De Blake, and devise the means to set him at liberty. I will not go where my mother is, but we will now go to the prison and seek an interview with the prisoner."

CHAPTER XV.

Dark was the fate that seemed to hang over the destiny of the poor but innocent De Blake. No one was allowed to enter his cell but his keeper, and consequently he was startled from a short slumber by the announcement of two strangers. They were no other than Henry and Zed, who had bribed the jailor to let them have a word with the prisoner.

"You are the unfortunate who is confined here for the crime of murder," said Henry. "What have you to say for yourself in answer to this dreadful charge?"

"I have said all an innocent man could say —no more than I believed to be true."

"We are friends come to offer you consolation. We would assist you to bear up against the great trial that awaits you."

"I am glad of friends; but what want you of me?"

"We would have you confess your crime, that God may pardon you, and prepare you for your doom. It is an awful thing to die without hope," added Henry, in a graver tone.

"It is indeed sin—but to confess what I know nothing of, would not be confession. I have only to say I am innocent."

"But have you no connection with this affair directly or indirectly.

"I have had a connection with it—but I am innocent. The confession I might make, as I have no evidence to clear me, would in my critical situation only reflect more to the proving I am guilty."

"But you must not withhold this, sir. It may be the very evidence that will save you."

De Blake then related to the stranger all the particulars of the supposed murder, which have already been described.

"This is enough," said Henry, "You are innocent I believe, and we shall endeavour to make the most of it in effecting your release, and proving your innocence."

"Thanks, sir; may heaven direct you."

Having ascertained all they wished, the strangers took their leave of De Blake.

"We shall be able to effect his release, Zed, or at least to prove his innocence with regard to the murder of my mother," said Henry.

"Yes," said Zed, "I recollect, now that he mentioned it, of seeing the dagger in Sinford's hand when he went out of the house."

"This you can swear to, Zed."

"My Bible oath on it," said Zed.

"This buckle shows that the ghost was a material one, as it also shows another passed, that it knocked you down by your running into it."

"Another proof who it was," said Zed, "by it's name being on the buckle."

"Name?"

"Yes, Sinford's name. He must have been the ghost, for he appeared next morning with one buckle."

"You saw him."

"I did. He questioned me as to whether I had found one between his house and De Blake's. I said no. I did not dare to mention where I found it, or let him know I had found one, as the ghost made me swear never to mention a syllable of what happened that night."

"You kept your oath strictly till you convinced yourself that it was not a ghost?"

"Yes."

After thus scanning the matter to their satisfaction, Henry and Zed took up their lodgings in the village to await the day of trial.

Henry was now a graduate from college, and the profession of law he had become proficient in. He could comprehend the most complex part of it, and he determined to appear as counsel for De Blake.

CHAPTER XVI.

THE day arrived. The jurors were set, and all the proof that could be had was brought forth necessary to condemnation. Sinford, with a brazen front—with a lie upon his tongue—arose and gave his testimony of what he knew, which seemed conclusive to the court.

The evidence for the defence was called for. The court was silent for some time, when Henry at length arose and addressed the court as follows:

"Gentlemen of the Jury,—There appears in this transaction a mystery that remains yet to be unravelled before you are to decide upon the point of life or death. I am a stranger to you, but I am no stranger to the wronged, and claiming the right to do good wherever I can, and having an interest in the prisoner, I have taken upon myself the obligation to defend him in this extremity. To proceed, I wish the witness who has just left the stand to resume it."

The court was astonished with the manner and tone in which this speech was uttered; and Sinford, as he resumed the stand which he had just left, began to tremble.

"Your name is Sinford?" asked Henry.

"Yes, sir."

"And resided once near De Blake's?"

"Yes, sir."

"You were there on the evening the travellers called at his house?"

"I was, sir."

"What was your business?"

"Merely a friendly call."

"Nothing passed in the evening about a dagger?"

"Nothing."

"Did any one enter the room while you and De Blake were in conversation?"

"No, sir," answered Sinford, a little confused.

"At what hour did you return home?"

"About nine o'clock."

"You stated before that two travellers stopped at De Blake's in the evening about six; that you were there; that the lady fainted on seeing De Blake."

Henry now begged leave that the court would listen to his evidence, and Zed, after being called to the stand in the usual manner and sworn, stated facts which made the eyes of many start from their sockets, especially those of Sinford, who rose with rage, and boisterously exclaimed that it was false.

"It is not false," exclaimed a female, rushing into the court-room.

"Gentlemen of the Jury," said Sinford, "this is a plot against my life. I affirm that it is false."

"Oh, thou wicked and perjured man. Deny it if thou canst—deny it to the woman whom thou hast so wrongly used."

"What dost thou mean—who are you, woman?"

"Look upon this scar, which you made with your own hand, and then ask me who I am," she said gently to the jurors; "the identical woman who was supposed to be murdered. You are not Sinford, but William De Blake, the brother of yonder innocent man."

A stillness followed this annunciation that could be audibly felt. They all gazed upon the woman with breathless astonishment.

At length the judge arose and said—

"Although the prisoner at the bar is exonerated from this supposed murder, another still lies upon him.

"The trunk or skeleton found buried on his land, beneath the tree, must be cleared before his liberty is assured. For this he was arrested, and must answer for it. The court will now proceed to the business."

This seemed a death-blow to all that had been done for poor De Blake. Henry knew not what to do, and Zed looked upon him, as he sat near him, expecting that he would say something.

The court was about to adjourn, when the old Indian Noman, who had been crouched down in one corner, advanced toward the stand, and stated in the following words:—

"Me know something about the killed

man. Me had been in the parts scarce two moons, before any white man was here, when me got into a quarrel with my squaw and kill her. Me buried her there. Me was sorry for it, for me love her ; but me was mad, then me no think of love, but mad. Me have lived here ever since. Me no go with my tribe ; me no like the world not at all. Me was going over the meadow one night. Me know that lady lying on the ground. Me have compassion and take her up, and carry her to my hut, and keep her from dying. The wound in the heart no heel till she be well."

This was enough to clear De Blake, and he was set at liberty, and the wicked Sinford took his place, and was remanded to prison to await his trial for an attempt to murder. The court had no jurisdiction over the Indian, as the crime was committed before the settlers came to that part of the country.

CHAPTER XVII.

IN the first place, the joy that Ella De Blake experienced at her father's release, and his absolute innocence established by a disclosure of before unseen facts, was inexpressible. So, also, was that joy felt by the mother at the restoration of her long lost son, and the son, at the restoration of the long lost mother. Zed had now made a favourable impression upon the heart of Dorothy, who, instead of slighting him, courted him as if afraid that she should lose him, while her mother rubbed her hands for joy that she was to have so likely a son-in-law, and she congratulated Mrs Stanwood that she had at last found that comfort the restoration of her son afforded her.

De Blake and his daughter were again happy, but as yet were ignorant to whom they owed their thanks for this timely interference.

They were seated one fine evening, as usual, at their window expressing their joys and wish to know who their benefactor was when he suddenly entered.

De Blake arose, and bowing slowly presented a seat, at the same time introducing his daughter—Ella, who blushed deeply and seemed confused at something she knew not what, and she chided herself for this awkward conduct.

At length she said, "Sir, we owe you much for your kindness."

"Nothing more than I presume you may abundantly pay," replied Henry.

"How, sir?" asked the father.

"By giving me your daughter's hand in marriage!"

Henry then made himself known, and De Blake willingly gave his consent to their union. A fainting of joy came over Ella at the discovery, and she fell swooning in Henry's arms.

It was a few weeks after the above circumstances that Mr De Blake was requested by a messenger to visit Sinford in his cell, when he confessed to him that he was his brother William, and had thus concealed his name that he might seek revenge on him for the affray that took place on his father's premises, and adding that he still believed him guilty of an attempt to murder him, and would hear no confession to the contrary from De Blake. He declared that he was innocent of the charge for which he was arraigned and convicted.

CHAPTER XVIII.

As we leave the Green mountain we proceed to the city of Boston—Boston as it was before the revolution—not bearing the gorgeous appendages it does now. The bright sun had gone down, and twilight had grown dim.

Boston harbour on this evening was very beautiful.

But only one vessel could be seen, which, we observe, is very peculiar in its rig. Her masts inclined much toward the stern, and were rather stunted. Her spars were very long, and calculated to carry a heavy press of sail. She was painted black, with a scarlet band running around her waste, and with red lining to her port-holes which are raised, displaying eight guns to a side. Her bulwarks were very high—as high as a man's head, and her hammock nettings were stowed like those of a man-of-war. She sat very low in the water, and was very sharp in the bows; her model was exquisite, and moulded with taste and symmetry. She was about two hundred tons burden, and presented no poop-deck, being flush fore and aft.

Her decks were neatly kept from rubbish, and clean, the rigging was coiled upon deck in the most tasteful manner; her scuppers were clean, and shone bright as polished brass. A small swivel gun was mounted in a superb manner upon the taffrail, and one of a like description upon her bow, we observe, and a Long Tom amidships. In short, she presents a most formidable appearance, as though she were fitted for a tough engagement as well as skimming the water with bird-like speed.

Upon her quarter deck are standing two persons leaning over her side, watching the fading tints of twilight, and the silver moon just peeping from the opposite horizon.

One's visage seems light, and his features those of an American, while the other had huge black whiskers, and the complexion and features of a Spaniard.

"This, you say, is the place of your birth," said the Spaniard.

"Yes," replied the American, "I was born in this country."

"It's reasonable to suppose that the sight of one's native land should inspire us with feelings such as we have experienced in our youths."

"Ah! Pedro, it might have been to me yet a land of happiness—but alas!—no more of this," he added, quickly; "these emotions are not deserving of me. I must cherish those of an opposite character."

"What place is yonder town?" asked the Spaniard.

"Boston," said the Captain. "It is some forty miles further into the country I wish to proceed—the journey I was speaking about yesternight."

"Can you perform it without danger?"

"Perfectly; with this cloak wrapped around me I can conceal all traces of my profession."

"As you are a pirate in disguise," exclaimed Pedro, "you would do well to wear a citizen's hat."

"Pedro," said he at length, "I am not in the humour now for jesting. Let the boat be lowered and manned, and I will take advantage of this bright moon and be off."

The boat was lowered and four men leaped into it, and like an arrow it bounded over the silvery surface of the waters.

CHAPTER XIX.

RANGER SINFORD, after he had, as he thought, effected the ruin of Henry Stanwood, followed him to the city, without, however, knowing whither Henry had gone. Here he plodded on in the low circle he had chosen, and soon was without the means of living, his father refusing longer to furnish him with supplies.

The love which he had cherished for Ella De Blake served to withdraw him from his reforming determinations, inasmuch as he now felt a spirit of retaliation and revenge; that she had refused him flatly to longer receive his addresses, and moreover charging him with the design, and sole conspirator, of involving Henry in trouble through a spirit of avarice.

All plans failing to procure him the means to subsist on, he, with another of his own colour in thought and reputation, resolved on pilfering and robbing.

These two accomplices in crime entered the

store of the rich firm with which Henry was connected, the result of which the reader is already acquainted with.

The poor wretch who was shot, luckily for Ranger, was his companion. He escaped justice, and in fear left the city. He shipped on board a vessel in the harbour, and sailed for the West Indies, in which place he remained for two years in quietness and tranquillity—the fright of the encounter and the overthrow he met with in Boston operating as a restraint upon any designing plots of mischief in his mind. His winning and ingenious address won for him in that place of fashion and gaiety, Havana, a circle of rich and warm admirers.

But his honours were almost invariably bestowed on one fair Senora, Isabella del Cascara.

It was in her father's family that the distinguished foreigner, our hero, the famous Monsieur de Allaha, was invited gratuitously to take up his quarters.

Upon the fair Isabella he placed his affections, and received a favourable hearing. She was beautiful beyond description.

"You have assured yourself of the full consent of my father you say, my dear Monsieur," said the little beauty, as they one evening sat in the drawing-room of Don Cusca's splendid mansion.

"I have, sweet," he said; "and now for yours, which remains the only barrier to the consummation of our happiness. Speak and all is cleared away."

"Some future time," interrupted she, "we may presume to talk of decision."

CHAPTER XX.

THE fortunes of our adventurer were, as he feared, to be turned to his disadvantage.

One evening he was ready, as he thought, at the appointed time. He waited anxiously in the drawing room for the appearance of Isabella, but she appeared not.

It was now dark, and Ranger made his way through the lighted streets with all possible speed, and was soon at the entrance of a saloon. He mounted the stairs, and a few more steps brought him to the hall.

The evening wore away, he led to the floor every beauty in the whole assembly, but nothing was to be seen of Isabella.

In the midst of his wanderings he cast a careless eye into the hall, and, to his amazement, he beheld the beautiful and lovely creature of his thoughts waltzing with a gallant Spanish gentleman. He started to his feet in amazement; could he believe his own eyes? could that be Isabella? He turned away in a fury, his passion rose almost, so as to be observable by the company. Smothering his almost bursting heart, which filled with horrible epithets, until the waltzing was over, he very deliberately took the Spaniard aside, and impudently asked—

"What are your intentions with yonder lady?"

"Insulting scoundrel!" exclaimed the

Spaniard in a rage, and loud enough to be heard all over the saloon. "Withdraw what you have dared to insult me with, or I'll demand satisfaction."

"I demand a proper answer to my question, as I am most intimately concerned in her behalf."

"Whose?" exclaimed the Spaniard. "Isabella de Cascara's did you say?"

"Aye, did you not hear me?" proudly replied Monsieur. "Isabella de Cascara."

"Hell and fury," he exclaimed at these words, and he laid his hand upon his throat, but he was prevented from doing violence by the intervention of several gentlemen, who separated the two, so hostile to each other, until their rage should be quelled.

The party now dispersed in the utmost confusion, with many wonderings and surprise among those unacquainted with the point of difficulty between the distinguished gentlemen.

Monsieur was much chagrined at this unexpected turn in affairs.

He resolved not to go again to Cascara's house until he had justified the matter to his perfect satisfaction; and accordingly took up his lodgings in the *Hotel de Caffa* for the night. As the Spaniard had taken to himself the protection of Isabella, he made no attempt to gain an acceptance to accompany her home, but at a distance dogged them to their home. Monsieur observed as they reached the door of the mansion, and were alighting from the carriage, that they remained at the door on the outside in earnest conversation. He drew near, and the substance he understood as follows :

"Isabella," said the Spaniard, "what am I to make of what I have heard and experienced to-night?"

"Do not speak as if you would chide ; as if you thought I had been unfaithful to you in your absence, Bernardo!"

"Ah, Isabella, what shall I think—you— no, could you—what claim has he, that he dares thus to insult Bernardo del Corpo. You know him."

"Hear, Bernardo," replied she, catching him by the arm and drawing him to her, as he had stepped back in the earnestness of his expression. "But my father bade me do thus!"

"How may I be assured of this, Isabella?" asked Bernardo, still doubting her credulity, and yet inclined not to. "Would you marry me at all hazards?"

"That I would, even if my father persisted.'

"Then will I still love you ; thou art again my dear, my adored Isabella."

He now embraced her, and imprinting a hearty kiss upon her forehead, which made the heart of our Monsieur, who was within hearing almost burst. So he muttered a few oaths by the way of cursing his own cowardly disposition, and soon reached his own lodgings.

He entered his room, and resolved upon a mode of revenge.

"I'll fight a duel with him. I shall engage him. I can trust to my abilities with the broad sword, or small one ; I'll try it at least. Such insult I will not brook."

He sat down to his table, and, seizing a pen and paper, wrote a challenge, and immediately despatched a courier with it.

CHAPTER XXI.

BERNARDO DEL CORPO was the son of a respectable and wealthy merchant in Havana. He had been cradled in the lap of wealth, and educated in a manner the great means his father afforded.

He was exceedingly handsome in appearance. He was the *beau ideal* of the most fashionable circles. Such was the person and character of Bernardo del Corpo, the rival of our pretending Monsieur, and the true lover of Isabella del Cascara.

Nothing could exceed the mortification which followed when the parents discovered the affection that was springing up between their children.

Bernardo was sent to Europe, where he remained some five years, and it is at his return that we have introduced him to the reader.

Bernardo sat in his chamber on the evening we have mentioned above, and after the events related, pondering upon them with no little excitability—his honour had been grossly insulted, and he felt he could not brook such control.

He was just on the point of taking his pen in hand when his servant entered, handed him a letter, and retired.

This was found to be a challenge from Monsieur De Allaha, which he at once accepted.

As the morning sun gilded the steeples and played upon the thousands of masts with which the harbour was filled, presenting the appearance of a dry forest, Bernardo was at his post; his servant for his second; for he needed no other, being well assured that he would kill his man. He took no surgeon. All was silent, when his servant informed him that his opponent had arrived. They then drew up, and prepared for a severe encounter, which gave the Frenchman every advantage, who ran him through the body; and the young Spaniard, uttering a fearful groan, fell pale and weltering in his gore.

"It's finished!" said our Monsieur to his second; and, turning upon his heel, walked deliberately away, with as much composure as if he had killed a dog.

Isabella del Cascara, as soon as the news reached her of Bernardo del Corpo's death, in a fit of passion made her way to the hotel occupied by Monsieur De Allaha. Armed with a dagger, she noiselessly gained admittance to his chamber, and would have inflicted dire revenge had not the Monsieur, by a dexterous movement, eluded her blow and made his escape.

Many were the investigations made for the apprehension of the murderer of Bernardo, who was well known and much respected; but the Monsieur soon made these of no avail by his speedy departure for sea in his piratical schooner.

Cruising one day off the coast, on the borders of which De Blake's farm was situated, Monsieur De Allaha, or, as he is better known, Captain Ranger Sinford, determined, with the aid of two or three of his desperadoes, to abduct the fair Ella, and in this vile purpose he was successful.

About the time these events were occurring, Henry Stanwood, in the isolation and hard studies to which he was subjecting himself, prior to his *debut* as a full-fledged lawyer, and more particularly because of his forced separation from her upon whom his heart was so fondly set, grew gloomy and despondent, and was advised by his medical attendant to betake himself to a sea voyage. This he at last consented to do, and left the port of Boston, in the hope of soon returning renewed in health and spirits.

For the first day or two after leaving port the canvas lay loosely against the masts, because there was no wind.

At last they reached the open sea, and a light breeze springing up, the noble craft, feeling the impulse, soon stood on her course.

The ship was bound to Havana, where she intended to take a cargo for Europe. A few more days had passed, and they were sailing down the eastern coast of Cuba with a fair wind. Nothing was to be seen above the horizon at sea, and the light breeze dashed them along with great rapidity. She had all sail set, expecting to drop into the harbour of Havana before dusk.

Henry amused himself now, and endeavoured to drown his thoughts by the novelty of the appearance of the country.

An hour had passed, and Henry mused uninterruptedly when he was roused to consciousness by the sound of—

"Sail, ho!" from the man at the look-out.

"Where away?" returned the captain, who had been pacing the quarter-deck, but now stopped suddenly to answer to the exclamations—

"Over our starboard quarter," returned the same voice at the look-out.

The stranger, notwithstanding the great speed of the Maria, gained miraculously upon her, and in an hour more she was within hailing distance, and all were startled with horror by a heavy voice bounding over the water from the stranger.

"What ship is that?"

"The Maria, of Boston," returned the captain. "What ship is that?" he added.

There was no answer; but at that moment a black flag was seen flying at the mast-head.

"Death's head and cross-bones!" exclaimed the captain, shivering. "Mr Mason, have the crew brought out; we must make a defence."

At this moment another sound rang in their ears from the pirate, in tones of command.

"Haul too, or I will fire into you."

The ship hove to; and the pirate run her bows in athwart the ship, just abaft the foremast.

All was now lost, for the pirates rushed on board like bees, and in a few moments the crew of the Maria, with her captain and mate, were heaped together on deck, though they sold their lives dearly, except one, Henry

Stanwood, who had done the work in that dreadful encounter of two ordinary men.

"Stand off," he shouted in tones of thunder, throwing himself into an attitude of defence that caused the pirates to stop in their advancement.

"Bravo! bravo!" shouted a voice from the piratical schooner who appeared by his attire to be the captain. "He is a brave fellow! spare him and bring him on board."

Henry could not have any great reluctance to this, and proceeded on board with the pirates, who took what specie there was on board, and then set fire to the ship. At sunset, the pirate was again lodged in her place of concealment.

About six or seven miles from Matanzas, among the huge beds of limestone that skirt the banks of a small river, is a cave of sufficient dimensions to admit a vessel, if her yards were hauled closely up, leading to a beautiful basin, where could repose a vessel in perfect security, without being discovered from the outside.

This was the harbour and concealment of the Sea Gull and her murderous crew. To this spot they immediately repaired, and dropped their anchor in the little bay after the capture of the Maria, and all proceeded in the boat to the cave whose entrance was visible after they were fairly within the basin.

"He is a royal fellow, Pedro," said Captain Blowell, "for we discover it to be him," referring to Henry, "he has energy enough to whip a whole ship's crew."

"Does he consent to become one of us?"

"He has made no serious objection, and I intend to have him initiated this very night, before he may have an opportunity to escape."

This conversation ensued between the captain and his mate.

Henry was that night taken and blindfolded, a rope tied about his wrists, and for a few moments left alone in total darkness.

Suddenly the bandages were removed from his eyes, and such a burst of splendour flashed upon him, that he could but believe that it was a transportation to heaven; but these thoughts were soon put to flight by his observing, kneeling in every direction around him, men clothed in red, their heads turned towards a kind of throne, upon which was seated a female form, her dress covered with innumerable diamonds sparkling in the light. By the melancholy cast of her countenance he could but fear some awful fate was to befal her. She was exceedingly beautiful, and his pity was already moved in her behalf. As he stood gazing upon her, a door opened in the opposite wall and another female entered, not so handsome in her countenance as the first, but more masculine in her proportions and outline of features. She walked firmly and quickly up to the trembling female upon the throne, and taking her by the hand led her to the floor, and asked her in a low voice, but loud enough for Henry to hear, "Do you still persist in your obstinacy?"

The maiden, as she appeared, merely bowed in affirmative.

Taking a sword, she led the victim towards Henry till within some five or six paces, where she stopped and spake to him.

"Do you still swear to abide by the oath you have taken to consecrate your life and services to the will of the evil one?"

"What wouldst thou have me do?" asked Henry, earnestly.

"Take this sword," said she at length, presenting him with the handle, "and this hand," she added, leading the girl nearer. Henry felt all the horrors of his situation, and at these words his blood chilled in his veins. He stretched out his hand and took the sword, and the other to grasp the fair hand stretched towards him. He shivered in every joint. He could not move.

"This is the test of thy steadfastness," said the woman, "the red bank the mark for thy sword. Strike and thou art true; but refuse and all the tribe of hell shall be upon thee."

All was silent. Henry glanced around him, and discovered among others the features of the captain. He knew not whether to obey or not. Who could his victim be? Some miserable female unfit to live, or one innocent and virtuous.

While thus reflecting, the lovely creature, lifting her face from the ground, whither it had been bent until now, in a disconsolate but clear tone, said—

"Despatch me quickly—this delay is worse than death!"

Henry seemed startled at this willingness to die, and the tone of her voice operated like magic upon his nerves. He thought he had heard it before. He stared wildly upon her.

"It cannot be Ella," whispered Henry.

"Henry!" reiterated she, in the same tone of voice.

"'Tis she!" exclaimed the astonished and overjoyed Henry, clasping her in his arms.

"Thy Ella, Henry," she exclaimed, at the same moment rushing towards him.

At this unexpected turn in the affairs, the men all started to their feet, and the captain rushed towards the loving pair with a loud exclamation for them to desist.

"Stand off!" exclaimed Henry, his voice echoing like thunder in his ears. "Is it thus," he added, turning to the captain, "you would implicate me in crime? Murder my own bride! Villain!"

"Lay hold of him!" shouted the captain, drawing his sword and advancing.

"Now for the disputed power!" shouted Henry, as the captain fell groaning to the ground with an incision through his body in the region of the heart. Bereft of their leader, the men dared not venture any further attack —they had been daunted before, and they dared not lift their arms to strike a blow.

Seeing that all hostile appearances were at an end, Henry turned his attention to Ella, who had swooned away and fallen to the ground. Raising her in his arms, he soon restored her to consciousness.

Henry found himself the sole master of all that belonged to Captain Blowell.

He took what treasure he wished for, and

in the course of two weeks the happy Henry landed on the wharf at Boston with the lovely Ella by his side.

Ella had informed Henry of her usage while in the hands of the Pirate, and who he was—Ranger Sinford—and that it was a custom with the league, on the initiation of a new member, to sacrifice a female to test their unflinching fidelity.

De Blake sunk under the weight of his woes, and died when his daughter was on her way to revive him.

Before his decease, he had recovered his property. Old Sawyer Grubb, with whom the administration of the property of Sinford had been entrusted, acknowledged, on his deathbed, that the papers which were the points of dispute between the neighbours, were forged by his own hand at the request of Sinford.

In due time Henry and Ella were united in the old but beautiful farm-house where they had first seen each other. They, however, returned to the city, giving to Zed and Dorothy the farm for their fidelity to Mrs Stanwood.

THE MAGIC FIGURE-HEAD;

OR,

THE LADY OF THE BLUE AND THE GREEN.

BY

CAPTAIN CAREY, U.S.N.

THE
MAGIC FIGURE-HEAD;

OR,

THE LADY OF THE BLUE AND THE GREEN.

CHAPTER I.

I'm a great sinner, reader, a *graceless* one at least, for I never say "grace" before dinner; and on the same principle when I spin a yarn, I don't intend to write a preface to it, for if it is good, preface won't better it any; if it is bad, a preface won't save it from your condemnation; so here we go, all sail set, sheets flowing and colours flung out, off upon a cruise.

Did you ever see Hurl Gate, or Hell Gate, as the old Knickerbocker Dutchmen used to call it (a place in the Sound, at the upper end of New York), when its ever-boiling "pot" is running over, mad with the effects of a regular north-east gale? If you have not, you have missed a sight, as the girl said to the countryman who hadn't seen the elephant.

Our yarn commences in the month of November, 1778, a time when our noble forefathers were fighting like tigers to secure the rights and liberties which we now, with but too little gratitude, enjoy. The trees were now nearly stripped of their "yellow sheen," and the wind whistled through their branches, as it would through the rigging of a " '74." The hour was midnight. Upon a point which stretches out just at the southern entrance of Hurl Gate, forming the outer part of a small cove which lies hidden almost entirely from the Sound, to the westward of the "Gate," stood a short, thick-set man, one who, like the body of French wit, was as *broad* as he was long. His dress was a mixture of the sailor's and landsman; his grey hairs were covered with a tarpaulin hat, a thick pea-jacket of home-made woollen, coloured with butternut bark, enveloped the upper portion of his form, while the lower part was encased in tight knee-breeches of the same; low-quartered shoes, with large brass buckles, covering his feet, which, indeed, were *feet*, mechanically speaking.

He was a huge, hardy-looking customer, one whose red face, wrinkled and scarred considerably, seemed like a map of character; his small, but very bright grey eyes, peered out from a cliff-like brow, and his rough beard, of perchance a week's growth, stuck out, like the quills of a young porcupine, in all directions.

In his mouth there was a short stump of a pipe, from which he ever and anon drew a hearty puff of smoke, which, for the moment, would wreath about his face like fog around a rock, and then vanish.

In one hand he carried a large, knotty cudgel; in the other he held a lantern—not one of our modern "globes," but a big tin lantern, with a door of isinglass, through which considerable light was reflected from a fat tallow candle, which occupied the socket within. As he stood under the thick branches of the trees on this point, he held the door of the lantern to the south, where the East River, for a long stretch, was entirely open to view, from his location, when it was light enough to see it.

"Dunder and blitzen, but it's tam'd cold," said our friend, as he shrugged up his shoulders, and bending down seemed to look along the water to the south. "If dat Captain Ballentine can peat his schooner up against such a wint, den Hans Nipperhausen—— eh! is dat a light on de water?"

The worthy Hans Nipperhausen bent once again low down toward the ground and scanned the gloom to the southward, where a small light like a star, low down with the horizon, could be seen, and after intently gazing at it some time, raised up, and again muttered, "Yes, it is a light, and it must pe he, for nopody put a man in love—or in liquor—would come nigh Helle-gat such a night as this. I must go to de point, for it'll pe tam close work for him to get in to-night."

As he said this, our Dutch friend walked down upon the extreme point of black rocks, so close that the surf dashed up against his body, and held the light clear up in view. In the meantime, the light which, in the distance, had at first nearly borne south from him now seemed rapidly to pass off to the eastward, but in a few moments it seemed again to move to the west, thus showing plainly that it was on board of a vessel, and that the vessel was beating up against the wind.

And now the query would be, what was she that could thus pass up through a channel occupied by the cruisers and gun-boats of the English, who at this time held New York and its environs: and why she had a light in her bows, which was so shifted at every tack that it could only be seen from the northward and not from the city, or any vessel that might be at anchor in the river astern.

But leaving these fancies for a moment, we will take a look at a building which stands upon the crest of a hill which overhangs the cove, about five hundred yards back from the spot where we left Hans Nipperhausen standing with his lantern.

It is an olden-time looking stone house, and is the residence of Mynheer Dietrich Van Twiller, who is the son of old Wouter Von Twiller, who originally owned all of Manhattan Island, which he purchased of the Indians for the merest trifle.

Let me introduce to you Katrine Van Twiller, the only daughter of Mynheer Dietrich. She is sitting alone in a little room, which forms a gable that overlooks the cove of which we have spoken. There is a neat little work-table by her side, on it stands a candle, which is so placed as to front the window. It is possible that this disposition of the light is intentional, for she ever and anon gazes out of the window, with a look of impatient anxiety, peering through the branches which grow so close that they could be reached by her hand. She evidently is expecting a visitor.

Katrine, though not a beauty, according to the usual taste of the world, is a very fine-looking girl. Her form, indeed, is very perfect; it is full, very plump, yet well-shaped. Her close-fitting sleeve displays a large, but finely-rounded arm; her dress closely-fitting, shows a full and noble bust, which, in its swelling proportions, denote that she has arrived at the age of womanhood; as she bends forward to look out of the window, she exhibits a foot and ankle which might be gazed upon with envy by many a southern belle.

As we before said, she is rather large, but her size is so well-proportioned, that it only adds to her beauty.

She shuddered as she heard the harsh whistling of the heavy gale, and as once more she looked out into the gloom she murmured—

"It will be impossible for him to come in to-night, the wind is so heavy, and it is very dark. Even Han. Nipperhausen's lantern could not help him much on such a night as this."

Her accent was slightly German as she spoke, but her words were purely English, as if her education had been well attended to.

"It is useless to hope, it is now so late," sighed the lady, as she started at the sound of the time-teller; "he could not get in, and perhaps it is best. Yet he wrote me he would be here to-night!"—and again the maiden sighed as if her heart was running over with the disappointment.

As she sighed, something very like an echo to the sound caused her to start suddenly and turn round toward the door of her apartment, and as she did so, she found herself in the arms of—a man.

We doubt not but she would have screamed with afright or surprise, but the intruder pressed his lips so closely to hers, in a long, warm kiss, that she had no chance to do so, and as she gazed upon him with her large, blue eyes, she did not attempt to escape from his embrace, therefore we may infer that he was not an unwelcome visitor.

As soon as he withdrew his lips from hers, while yet her face was suffused with rich blushes, she exclaimed,

"Oh, Hunt, how could you do so? You are enough to frighten one to death."

"You don't seem much frightened, dearest," replied the person whom she addressed, who was a fine-looking young man, nearly six feet high, with an elegant figure, hair curling and jetty black, and fine expressive features; "but you were sighing so sadly when I entered, that I thought I would frighten the *blues* away if possible."

"I was sad, dear Hunt, because I thought you would not come to-night, the weather was so stormy and the night so dark———"

"That made it only more safe and easy for me to keep my promise. I've slipped by the enemy without being discovered at all; and my noble little schooner, the 'Ocean Queen,' lays in the cove down here as safe as if there wasn't an English frigate afloat, and besides, if you know Hunt Ballentine, you know him to be one who never waits for wind or tide when his promise is given."

"I know you are punctual, dear Hunt, but how is my brother—is Karl well, will he ever make a sailor?"

"He's as good a sailor now as ever trod a plank."

"But is not Karl coming on shore?"

"No; he preferred not; he told me to give his love to you, and this kiss," replied the other, bestowing the latter upon the lips of his fair companion, and then adding—

"You know, dearest, that I have only a couple of hours to stay in here; I must be out of this before daylight comes on, to show my 'Ocean Queen' to the English bull dogs—they have been on her track so often that they know her but too well."

"Yes, and I fear that that knowledge may yet lead to her capture and your destruction. Do you keep that large painting on her sail yet, which marks her as far as she can be seen?"

"Just lend me a light a minute, and I'll show you," replied the sailor, leading her toward the window.

Three times he raised the light to the window, and each time passed it out of sight, and then in a few moments after replaced it as it was.

At this moment the bright glare of a blue light gleamed up from the deck of a vessel in the cove, showing for a time, as clear as day. each rope and object upon her spars and about her decks. She was a fore-topsail schooner, with masts very taut and raking; her fore-topsail clewed up, her foresail in the brails, and her head sails hauled down. Her mainsail was hoisted, and on it could be seen painted in full size, and at full length, the semblance of a woman, one strangely like Miss Katrine.

From the mast head of this vessel waved a red flag, having the words, "Ocean Queen," embroidered in silver upon it—from her gaff fluttered the flag of our country.

"Isn't she a beauty?" said the young commander, as he gazed at his schooner with pride. "I gave them directions before I left to show her to you, if I made signal to them. Do you see Karl?—he stands there by the helm—see, he waves his sword to us."

"Yes, I see him," replied the sister; "and your vessel is indeed beautiful."

"She would be far more beautiful to me, if my Katrine was there in person to share my cabin," replied the other; then again pointing toward his vessel, he added, "You don't observe my new figure-head, Katrine. It is one that I had put upon her when I was in Cherburg, last cruise, and it is a curious piece of work."

The maiden now gazed more closely upon it, and observed that it was the statue of a woman of very large size, not standing out clear of the bows of the vessel, as figure-heads generally do, but set right in the cut-water, or, in fact, forming it.

This, too, at the distance, seemed to look like her; and as she gazed upon it she said,—

"What a singular taste you have, Hunt; but in what is it so curious this new figure-head of yours?"

The young captain smiled as he said,—

"My men say that it is bewitched, for when we come in shore her eyes turn green, her face is paler, and she wears an angry look, but when we turn our prow to seaward, and get an offing, her eyes again become as blue as your own, and she seems satisfied!"

"But you don't believe such nonsense!" said Katrine.

He smiled again, and simply answered,—
"Sailors are very superstitious, you know!"

When again they looked toward the vessel, the blue light was extinguished—nothing could be seen in the gloom to indicate her presence—nothing heard save the whistling gale.

CHAPTER II.

THERE yet stands an old building, just back of the Battery, in New York, which, at the time our history commences, was occupied as "quarters" by a number of British officers.— Here, at all hours, one could hear the clattering of wine glasses, and the laughter of wild and careless men; until the small hours of the morning could be heard their festive songs and shouts of revelry—many and deep were their carousals.

They gambled, and drank, and sung their time away, as garrisoned soldiers but too often do, even in the present day.

At the table—on an occasion when occurred

the following incidents—there were many of the army and a few of the naval officers present, and they seemed half-seas over.

The sailors were a little better ballasted than the others; and were, with one exception, more sober than their brethren of the other service.

This exception was a young man of twenty-four or five years of age; one who, were it not for the evident marks of dissipation upon his face, would be considered very handsome. He was tall, well-shaped, had eyes of keen but liquid black, hair of the same colour, features regular and noble—but his complexion was red with the stain of debauchery, and his eyes were sunken and his cheeks bloated. Let him be made known to you as Lieutenant Dorsey, of the Royal Navy.

The others seemed to be bent on making him drunker still, or, in professional parlance, determined to "lay him under the table," for, though he was now scarcely able to sit up, they called upon him for a toast.

Filling up his glass with some sparkling sherry, the young officer cried,—

"Here's Kate Van Twiller, the sweetest rebel and the prettiest girl in America!" and drank off his glass to the last drop.

"Kate Van Twiller!" was the universal cry of the rest, as they drank the toast, and then came the inquiry from one,—

"Who is she, Dorset?—where is your beauty? let us know, and give us a chance to judge for ourselves."

"I'll tell you who she is and where she is,

but blast my eyes! if any of you can get a peep at her. I've hard work enough to see her myself."

"Well, heave ahead and tell us where your paragon holds forth."

"She's the only daughter of a man that can call three millions his own at this hour, but you are right about my getting acquainted with her on one of my break-neck rides, as you call them."

"Do spin us the yarn," cried the others.

"Well, I will :—I was riding out up along the Sound shore of the island, about ten days ago, and was going at the rate of twelve or fourteen knots past an old Dutch mansion, just abreast of Hell Gate, when a big black Newfoundland dog jumps out from the gate way, right before my horse. He got scared, slewed himself round as quick as lightning, and landed me against a pile of rocks in such a way that I saw stars at noon-day. It knocked my senses out of me completely, and when they came to me, I found myself very comfortably stowed away in a nice bed, with a pretty girl in the room watching me. Well, as soon as she saw that I had come to, she slips off and calls her old father, and he and a Dutch doctor, a kind of family attendant, came in, and with their help I was soon on my feet again."

"Did you see her again?"

"Yes; but only once, for she was timid as a fawn, but she shall soon get used to the sight of me. I've been twice to see her, and both times she was excused by the old folks; but

I'll be d——d if I don't see her before long!"

"Bravo! old fellow!" cried several of the mess; "and you must introduce your friends—'Beauty and Booty' is our motto, you know."

"Well, I will, when I get her in train and properly broken in!" replied the other, and then added,—"I'd like to finger a million or so of the old 'un's dollars. It's a sin that they should lie idle."

"So it is," replied the rest; "can't you invent an excuse for confiscation, and let us go shares?"

"I don't know; but these old Dutchmen are deep as the ocean—you can't find them out. And the girl is a rebellious one I know, for she even looked at my uniform with a glance of hatred; and, after I had recovered from my fall, gave me as wide a wake as if I'd been a pirate."

"Well, if she's a rebel you must captivate her!"

"Just what I intend to do—she shall be mine, by fair means or foul, and that is what I swore when I first saw her, and you all know whether Frank Dorsey is a man to back from his determination!"

"Well, here's luck to you in another glass!" shouted the revelling crew—and again the young debauchee filled a bumper.

In a few moments he arose from the table and reeled to a sofa, whereon he tumbled and was soon wrapped in sleep. At last but two were left.

One of these was an elderly, very red faced individual—one who gave outward sign of being one of that peculiar class who never get blue; one whose very body seems to be of a spongy nature, enabling them to "soak up" any amount of liquor without feeling its effects. His uniform was that of a lieutenant in the navy; and his having arrived at no higher grade, although grey-headed, spoke not well for his character.

His companion was of the army, and as he pointed towards the stupified Dorsey, asked:—

"Who is that young fellow—Dorsey, I mean?"

"Well, Frank Dorsey is first lieutenant of the schooner 'Harpy;' he is the jolliest fellow on a spree, the best shot in a scrape, and the keenest dog on a woman's trail that there is on the station!"

"Truly, you give him a good character," replied the other; "but I mean, who is he at home?—who is his father, and what is his family?"

"Well, I've heard it hinted that a certain Count B., of French origin, who resides in England, sends him money, and got him promoted to his present situation. He never speaks of his parents, but he shot poor M'Keever for insinuating that one Miss P., of London, looked very like him, and was about old enough to be his mother; and I have heard that this Miss P. and Count B. were very fond of cruising in the same latitudes!"

"So, so!—and he is a regular **libertine**, duellist, and—does he gamble?"

"Yes, often; and he has the luck of the very devil! He won all my last month's pay!"

"Well, if men will play with fire, they must expect to get their fingers burned!" replied the other, and then added—"let us take another glass and adjourn!"

Bidding the other good night, he passed out from the room to go to his quarters. As he stepped out, he drew his martial cloak closely around his tall, manly form.

Just as he reached his own door a long, vivid flash of lightning lit up the river in his front, and to his surprise he saw a vessel scudding down before the gale under a very heavy press of canvas.

He got but a single glance at her, and could only note that she was an armed and well-manned topsail schooner, and that she was carrying a tremendous press of sail for such a blast, which he saw no necessity for, if she was not some vessel of the American fleet endeavouring to get to sea before the day set in.

While he was gazing, his suspicions and hopes seemed to be both realised, for the red flash of a gun glared in the gloom towards the "Narrows," and ere its dull report had reached his ear, another and then another showed that something was wrong upon the water.

Then soon after, signal rockets were seen streaming up in the air, and blue lights were shown from the different vessels, giving notice of a general alarm.

CHAPTER III.

At the close of our first chapter, we left Hunt Ballentine and Katrine Van Twiller enjoying a lover's *tete-a-tete* in her father's house, while the worthy old gentleman was sound asleep.

We will now return to them, some two and a-half hours having elapsed, which they have, we doubt not, spent very happily, in such converse as pure, warm loving hearts can best enjoy. We will break in upon them at the moment when the young captain arose and said—

"Dear Kate, I must be off. I've now stayed a full half hour over my time, and I must go. But good night. See, it is now almost dawn, and I've a regular gauntlet to run. You'll see me when the moon is gone, at this time next month, if I have to come in a row-boat. There now, good night." As the sailor said this, he pressed another warm kiss to her lips, and then, with a step as noiseless as that with which he entered, he left the room.

When he reached the door he found our old friend, Hans Nipperhausen, sleeping on the thick corn-shuck mat, where he had left him to act as sentinel. His lantern stood beside him, and being aroused, the old fellow arose, and with it proceeded to light the young captain down the hill side toward his vessel, through the thick undergrowth which grew upon the steep.

"A cold raw night is this, Hans," said the captain to the attendant as they hurried along.

"Here's something to buy some schnaps with, to keep you warm on such nights;" and the captain handed him a purse. "And Hans, you must be very careful never to say that you saw an American privateer come into Helle-gat cove at midnight, and sail again before dawn. It might give your master trouble."

"Hans never talks mooch," replied the man.

By this time the two had arrived at the water side, and here a boat, manned by six hard-faced old tars, lay ready for the commander. He sprang into it, and within another minute was standing upon the deck of his beautiful schooner.

As he put his foot over the gunwale, he cried,—

"Up anchor, Mr Barnacle—we've been here too long already."

"Aye, aye, sir," responded a rough, manly-looking person of about thirty-five or forty years, who was standing by the hatchway of the cabin, from which a light reflected upon his face and form, and then he added,—

"Hoist away the head sails—sheet home the topsail—loose top-gallan' sail, and let flow the main sheet!' And as those orders were obeyed, the schooner's bows gracefully fell off before the wind, and in a moment she was dashing out from the quiet little cove into the boiling waters of Helle-gat.

Guided by the lantern of Hans, who had hurried down to the point, they swept safely out into the East River, and now taking a compass course they headed down the bay.

"We must crowd the cloth on her, captain," said the first lieutenant, Barnacle. "We've but little more than an hour to daylight, and these flashes of lightning paint up the water entirely too plain for our safety."

"True," replied young Ballentine. "Give her the square sail and loose the main gaff topsail."

These sails were soon spread to the roaring blast, and with every spar bending and creaking with the weight of canvas, the beautiful vessel rushed swiftly through the foam.

The Battery, Governor's Island, Castle William—all were safely passed, and yet the dawn did not pale the east, thanks to the darkness of the storm, yet they were not out of danger, for in "the Narrows" below them lay a cordon of English vessels, which they had passed in going up, only by being taken for a tender to a "74," the Endymion, which was cruising outside the Hook.

"Keep a bright look-out on both bows and ahead," cried the watchful lieutenant; "and if you see anything, pass the word aft, in low tones to one another—we must keep as still as cats in a dark room."

"See that every light is extinguished, but have all ready for action," added the commander; and then turning to the young officer who stood at the helm, he said—

"You must be quick with the wheel, Karl, if we are hailed; if we run afoul of anything going at this rate, it would send us all to kingdom come!"

At this moment, while he was giving the caution, the word was passed from the bows:

"A light right ahead ! port your helm ! "

Quick as thought the helm was put aport, and the next moment they swept close past a fleet of vessels.

CHAPTER IV.

WE must now change the scene of our tale.

The mother country had hardly realised in its full force the momentous nature of the struggle which was then in progress—a struggle which caused Columbia to spring forth, armed *cap-a-pie*, like a lovelier and better Minerva, into the world.

Some of the denizens of Albion were, however, united by ties of kindred, friendship, or business very strongly to the young republic.

Among those who took an interest in the American war was the person whom we are about to introduce to our pages.

In his chamber, in an ancient castle on the sea-coast of England, that portion of which, under the name of Peveril's Point, juts out into the British Channel, sat a very singular-looking old gentleman ; one who, by purchase, had become the proprietor of the beautiful estate of Melcomb, on which was situated the old castle which we allude to.

The gentleman, by his grey hairs, pale and care-worn face, and attenuated form, seemed to be one who had felt many a rude gale in his life-cruise. which, according to his appearance, might have lasted some sixty-five years or thereabouts, though he was still erect in his carriage.

The height of his forehead, which was square, and not receding, coupled with the deep lines upon it, gave token that he was one whose mind was active, and his general appearance was intellectual and sage-like.

He was alone in his chamber, seated beside a table. reading a letter which he had just taken from a package which lay before him. His face was flushed, and the contents of the letter seemed anything but pleasing to him, for after perusing, he cast it down, arose angrily from the table, and commenced pacing up and down the room.

"So, so! This is the end of all my pains with that froward boy—he, a born nobleman, a descendant from a line of kings, has dared to side with a party who declare all men to be born 'free and equal.' It is strange that he so proud, so like myself, should so forget his birth and dignity. The next I hear, he will be hung as a traitor to the country in which he was born, or perhaps in battle fall a sacrifice to his madness. He must not remain there. I will recall him, and if he dare to refuse obedience I will disinherit him! What hath he to do with the quarrel between England and her colonies, and why should he side with the rebels?"

Still as he spoke, to and fro strode the old man, until at last he became more calm, and again approaching the table, rang a little bell which was upon it.

In a few moments a servant, an old grey headed man, opened the outer door, and approaching, said—

"You rang, my lord?"

"Yes, Ricard; I want your advice before I undertake a journey in my old age. I fear that it has become necessary for me to go to America. My boy, the son upon whom I have centred my very soul, out of some foolish freak of romance, has joined the rebels who are in arms against King George!"

"And what would you do, my lord?" asked the servant.

"Do, sirrah! I would reclaim him from his act of folly. He, an heir to the purest title that ever graced a noble name, turn into a Republican! No! it shall not be—he is my only son and——"

"Your only son, my lord?" and the servant emphasised deeply the words as he made this interruption.

"My only acknowledged son!" replied the nobleman; "why need you hint at another?"

"Because I thought my lord had forgotten him," replied the servant.

"No, Ricard, I have not forgotten him, nor he me, as will appear in a letter lying on the table, in which he asks me for five hundred pounds, giving as his reason that he has been promoted to a first lieutenancy, and his expenses thereby increased."

"It seems a pity, my lord, that Master Hunt had not entered the royal navy."

"It were better, than that he should be serving where he is now is," replied the other—"but I spoke of going to America."

"You wish to meet your son in person?"

"Yes, if it is possible."

"I think it would be impossible; there is no port wherein you could find him, I'll warrant, for the coast will soon be lined with his Majesty's cruisers."

"Well, what would you propose?—I must try to save him, and recall him from his error."

"Can you not send him letters?"

"How?—he is a rebel now; the king's mail would not be a proper conveyance."

"You can send it by private hand, and it can reach him."

"By whom? I think that no one could do it so well as myself."

"I could serve you as faithfully in this as I have in other things, my lord."

"You have been faithful and true, Ricard," said the nobleman, thoughtfully, "but I think in this case it would be better that we both should visit America together. We can adopt some safe disguise and remain unknown, while we make our plans and put them in operation."

"It is for you to order, my lord, and for me to obey," replied the servant, who, notwithstanding his apparent humility, seemed to have a wayward and wilful spirit.

"We will go," responded the other—"we will go, therefore make all the preparations as soon as possible. I will not lose my only son and heir without an effort to save him."

"Your *only* son!" said the servant, in an under tone, not heard by his master, as he turned to leave the room, and a singular sneer accompanied the remark.

We owe an apology, reader, for having left our hero, Captain Ballentine, and his beautiful clipper, the "Ocean Queen," in a scrape, and having left you in suspense regarding their fate.

When daylight came, they were yet inside of the Hook.

In their wake were several English ships and vessels of war, all making sail in chase; but for these, Ballentine had little care, he knew that he could outsail them. Yet his cheek grew pale and a shadow of anxious care darkened his face when he saw the white sails of a large line-of-battle ship loom up from just outside the bar, and he knew that her batteries would be a hard gauntlet to run, if, indeed, it were possible to get by her.

"What do you think of this?" said he, turning to Mr Barnacle, who, with his spyglass, had been very deliberately engaged in a general survey of their position.

"I think we're in a pretty bad box, but I have been in as bad before," replied the lieutenant.

"How are we to get out of it?"

"Run out of it, sir, of course, if we can— but that bloody shark outside the bar will be apt to bother us some."

"Yes, he may cut up our spars and disable her, and then we'll be taken."

"Not while the barkie swims, or I live, Captain," replied the other. "I don't want to find my berth in one of their rotten prison-ships; I'd rather slip my cable at once, and die like a man."

"You are right, my brave fellow; and never shall that flag come down while I have life. If they take us, they'll have to sink us first."

This conversation, unconsciously to the speakers, had been carried on in a tone sufficiently audible for the crew to hear it, and when their commander expressed the last sentiment, they burst out into a hearty cheer, which rang like a yell of defiance over the waters through which they were swiftly dashing.

The vessel outside seemed to have discovered them, for she now hoisted the ensign of St George at her gaff, and shook out the reefs in her topsails, as if to get her ready for working easily.

She also hauled close in to the bar, so as completely to shut in the "Ocean Queen," which vessel was too well known by all the cruisers on the coast not now to be recognised.

She was now standing right out for the English "74," whose distance was not more than a couple of miles, and there were several vessels still nearer in her wake.

The wind was on her larboard quarter, enabling all of her sails to draw well, and had it not been for the cruiser ahead, she could easily have escaped from those astern.

"I must do something to keep that fellow off out of gun shot," cried Ballentine, and then, as he glanced from one end of the bar to the other, a plan seemed to suggest itself to his mind, for he cried,—

"Man the braces, my lads, and stand by all the sheets. Be lively now, and don't let

go of a sheet or brace till I give the order.——
Round in the weather braces, slack off the sheets. Karl, head her off dead before the wind."

This manœuvre caused the vessel to head down the coast, and it now seemed to be her commander's intention to slip close along the beach, and by this means elude the larger vessel. The latter seemed to comprehend the idea, and instantly her helm was put up, more sail made, and she bore away to the southward, under a cloud of canvas, with a course to intercept the schooner.

"That's all right, she'll be a mile to leeward before she can take in sail and haul upon the wind!" cried Ballentine, while his face grew brighter. Then turning to Karl, he cried,—

"Hard down the helm, and luff her on a wind, my lad."

In a moment the schooner's course was changed, she heading right up along the Long Island shore, high enough to look through the "swash," or small channel at the northern end of the bar.

The "74" saw the new change in her course, and luffed as soon as possible, but, as Ballentine had predicted, she was so much more slow and unwieldy than the schooner, that she lost nearly two miles by the ruse, and now there seemed a chance of the latter getting out clear before the Englishman could regain his lost ground.

The ruse which he had been forced to adopt, while it bettered his position with his outside customer, had enabled the others to gain on him, and he saw that he was now within the range of two of them, one a schooner, nearly the size of his own, the other a fast sailing corvette, which had chased him before.

He had hardly noticed this when a shot from one of the bow guns of the corvette whistled by a few fathoms astern of him, dashing up the water as it ricochetted along, across the bar.

The old lieutenant looked at this and shook his head.

"Bad work this would be if one of their shot were to hit a spar," said he; and then, as if his words were prophetic, crash came another, and they saw their maintopgallantmast hanging by its rigging.

"Lay aloft and clear away the wreck—quick, my lads," cried the young commander.

"By the holy pipers but we may be thankful for those shot," cried Barnacle, as he looked over the side; "the schooner is going at least two knots faster now than before. She had too much canvas on her. I thought she laboured harder than she ought."

"So she is," responded Ballentine; "bear a hand, aloft there, and get in those flapping sails —keep her luff, Karl. One mile more and we can shut in the point and get clear of their fire."

Shot after shot from the pursuing vessels now whistled past them, but none struck her, and within five minutes the desired point was gained, and they were free from the shot of their pursuers for the time.

"What schooner was that in the chase?" asked Ballentine of his first lieutenant, after they had got everything secured and repaired again.

"The 'Harpy,' sir; she was built for a smuggler, but sold to the British Government when the war broke out."

"She shall be mine before another month's pay has become due to her officers," said Ballentine.

"How will you take her, when she keeps in port all the time, under the wings of the heavier craft? She never comes out to give you a chance."

"Then I'll take my chance inside with the boats, as I did with the 'Fire-fly.'"

"Sail ho!" cried the look-out from the forward cross-trees, at this instant.

"Where is she? Can you make out her rig?" asked the captain.

"She's a ship, sir, standing in for the land."

"A man-o'-war?"

"I can't see anything, sir, to show it—her sails don't look square enough."

"Well, keep a bright look-out on her, and report if you can make out anything else."

"Aye, aye, sir."

CHAPTER V.

WHEN the officers met at dinner on the day after the night in which occurred the debauch described in the third chapter, the subject of conversation was the daring venture of the

"Ocean Queen" into the harbour, and her subsequent escape.

"I wonder what reason her commander had for running such a risk?" asked the army officer whom we described as having been the last at the table on the preceding night. "I presume the fellow came in for some fresh grub."

"Well, I hope he got it," answered the other; "it would be a pity for him to take so much trouble for nothing. It seems strange to me that he should get away so easy."

"This is not the strangest of his escapes, by any means," replied Dorsey; "her captain is for ever doing some saucy thing or other. It was he that cut out the 'Fire-fly'—it was he that took the tender of the 'Endymion,' and then made a fire-ship of her, and came within an ace of burning the old '74' before her officers and crew smelt the rat. He has done more mischief than all the rest of the privateers on the coast."

"Why do you not take him?"

"His craft sails like a witch—he knows every inch of the coast, and you might as well chase the 'Flying Dutchman,' for he is about as hard to get hold of. But we'll have him yet."

"I should like to know why he came in on such a stormy night as last night was."

"Because it was the only time he could hope to pass our fleet safely; had he been an hour earlier in going out, perhaps he would never have been seen by our vessels at all."

"What could a privateer have that was important to any rebels near us?"

"News from France, perhaps; or she might have captured some ammunition with which to supply the rebels."

"That is true, but if she came in last night, she could not have gone far to get out again so soon."

"She may have been in the Sound for some time."

"No; she was reported as seen at sea but two days ago by the 'Orpheus,' which arrived yesterday. The frigate tried to catch her, but 'twas useless for her to try. The schooner left her as if she were at anchor."

"Some woman has perhaps led her brave skipper into the adventure. Men, you know, will risk more to see a pretty girl than for anything else. I've no doubt you'd let your horse throw you again to get a sight of your fair Katrine."

"I'll get a sight of her without that trouble," replied Dorsey, and then added—"I must go aboard this afternoon, and see how things work there. I ought not to have stayed ashore last night."

Although it was some fifteen miles distant from her, Kate Van Twiller had heard the first gun that was fired by the enemy when the "Ocean Queen" was discovered, for she had not retired to her bed after parting with her lover, but had waited with anxious suspense for the daylight to come.

When she heard that gun she sprang from her seat as if its report was a death knell to her hopes, and then, in agony, she listened for the rest. And as again and again she heard the distant sound, her tortured mind pictured her lover engaged in terrible and unequal conflict; she saw him bleed and fall in her terrified fancy, and the imaginary evil seemed worse than would have been a knowledge of the reality of her dreams.

But as she listened carefully each shot seemed to be farther off than before, and as the sound became more faint, the stronger grew her hopes that her heart's idol had escaped.

With the first glimpse of daylight, she despatched the faithful Hans Nipperhausen to the city to gain all the information he could for her.

"What is the matter, child?" asked her father, when he saw her come down, pale and with swollen eyes.

"Nothing, dear father, only I did not sleep well last night; there was such a storm, and I thought of poor Karl, and the rest who are upon the water."

"Karl had no business to go there. I told him to let the Yankees fight for themselves. You needn't cry for him;" and then, while he looked her sternly in the face, he added—"I believe you think more about that fool of a captain that coaxed poor Karl away. But you had better be looking out for somebody a little better than such as he,—without a dollar to bless himself."

"I feel little like looking out for any one, sir," replied the daughter blushing, "but if I did wish a husband, I should not look for a better than Hunt Ballentine."

"There it is!—I thought so!—the girl is in love with that good-for-nothing captain!" growled Mynheer Van Twiller to his wife.

"But it is of no use, girl—you can't have *him!* I'd sooner give you to the man who wrote to me, last night, about you."

"Wrote to you about me, father! What do you mean?"

"Read that letter, child," said the old gentleman, in answer, as he cast down a note on the table before her.

Her face grew red and pale, alternately, as she read it, and she murmured—

"An offer from one I have never seen but *once!* and he a man whose character is stamped on his face and written in his every action. Father, have you answered this letter?"

"No, girl, I have not yet; I only got it this morning."

"Then let me answer it?"

"What will you tell him, child?"

"That he has mistaken Katrine Van Twiller if he thinks the glitter of a gilt button can win her heart in a day—that I wish to see or hear of him no more."

"Well, that's right, and if you'll send the same kind to Captain Ballentine, if he sends or comes a courting you, it'll be better still."

"I will go and answer this note," said Katrine; and without having tasted of the food upon the table, she left the room.

On her way to her own chamber she met Hans. who had already got back from the city.

"What! back so soon, good Hans. What is the news?"

"De schooner had got out of de harbour safe before I left, and now she's all safe."

"Thank God! Now again my heart is lighter," exclaimed the fair girl.

The maiden seemed more calm now as she went to her chamber to answer the letter which, we will "confidentially" tell the reader —and nobody else—was a formal request from Frank Dorsey, to be admitted as a regular visitor at the house, and as a suitor for the hand of Katrine.

What her answer was, we may best infer from describing the scene of its reception and perusal by Lieutenant Dorsey, on the same evening.

He was seated in a private room in a hotel near the battery, when it was handed him, and bidding the waiter tell the messenger to wait until he had read it, he hurriedly broke the seal.

His face had beamed with pleasure when he first glanced upon it, but as now he scanned its contents, his brow grew dark with vexation and disappointment.

"So, so! the proud jade declines the honour of my visits—eh? By the beauty she possesses, but she shall pay for this insult. Will not even permit me to visit her—eh? I will soon learn her that I'm not a boy, to be put off with a word. *Declines the honour!* indeed."

With an angry curse upon his lips, the young officer tore the letter in strips, and then turning to the bell-rope of his room, rung it so violently that he broke it.

In a moment the waiter re-entered the room.

"Who brought this note?"

"A Dutchman, sir—a stupid sort of a fellow."

"Send him here, and bring me up a bowl here."

"Yes, sir," said the waiter, hurrying away to obey the order.

"I must make friends with the servant, if possible," soliloquised Dorsey; "he may be of use to me yet; at anyrate, I can find out something."

"You are the man who brought me this letter from the beautiful Miss Katrine, are you not?" asked Dorsey, in a kind, patronising tone.

"Yaas," was the brief reply of Hans.

"Well, here is a guinea for you," added the officer. "Take it, my good fellow. I'm willing to give you a guinea any time, for a letter from her hand."

Hans mechanically reached out his hand for the gold.

Lieutenant Dorsey then put a number of questions to the sagacious Hans, who answered evasively and in monosyllables, and at last prepared to depart, alleging that he was told to be quick.

Lieutenant Dorsey then said, "Tell your mistress that I was sorry my request was not complied with; but not a word of the questions. Do not say I asked anything about her, do you hear?"

"Yaas," replied the servant, and departed.

CHAPTER VI.

We will take up the end of our fourth chapter again, where we left the "Ocean Queen" with a sail in sight, and the query as to whether she was a friend or foe unsolved.

In about an hour from the time the look-out first descried the stranger, he again hailed the quarter-deck, saying that he thought the vessel in sight was an English armed transport.

"Does she show many teeth?" asked Lieutenant Barnacle.

"I can see but four port-holes of a side, sir," replied the man.

"Eight guns well served might rob us of some good men; we must try a ruse with her!" said Ballentine, and then hailing the look-out he asked,—"does she show her colours yet?"

"No, sir; but she's English—I know by the square cut of her sails, and her spars being all blacked."

The commander raised his spy-glass again to his eye, and, after looking attentively at her, he turned to his lieutenant and said,—

"Get the English ensign ready, Mr Barnacle; clap the patch over the 'Queen,' and stand by to pass our craft as the 'Harpy.' We must uniform ourselves again!"

"Aye, aye, sir! I'll soon fix the barkie, so that the devil wouldn't know her if he had even sailed in her."

In a short time the dashing "Ocean Queen," in appearance, officers, crew and all, seemed to be an English cruiser.

Meantime, the two vessels were rapidly

nearing each other, and Ballentine hailed through his trumpet in the usual manner,—

"Ship ahoy! what ship is that?—where bound to and where from?"

To which her red-faced old skipper answered,—

"The transport 'Supply,' Coldhound, master; from Portsmouth to New York, with stores for General Clinton!"

"Heave to, and I'll come aboard," responded Ballentine.

"What schooner is that?" now asked Capt. Coldhound, in turn.

"His Britannic Majesty's schooner 'Harpy,'" answered Barnacle in place of his commander, who appeared to be preparing to go aboard.

The master of the transport seemed to be satisfied, and luffing up a little ahead and under the lee of the schooner. hove his main-topsail aback, and left his craft almost stationary.

Meantime preparations were going on aboard of the schooner for a very pretty little manœuvre, which will not prevent us from listening to the remarks of two individuals on board of the 'Supply,' which seem to have a connection with our plot.

When the commander of the schooner first hailed them, the elder of the two, or he who seemed the elder, turned to the other and remarked,—

"Ricard, I surely have heard that voice before, and the 'Harpy!' That was the vessel to which the other, Frank Dorsey, wrote me he had been promoted. Surely it was his voice that we heard!"

"Most likely, my lord,—they are half-brothers, you know," replied the other.

"But I fear that he may recognise us—I do not wish to meet *him* here!"

In the meantime the schooner forged ahead and down upon the transport.

"Look out, sir, or you will fall aboard of me!" cried the captain of the transport, who thought the movement accidental.

"That's just what we want!" shouted Ballentine, as his vessel's bow struck the Englishman, and before the latter could reply, forty armed men were on his decks; and Ballentine, springing upon the deck before him, added,—

"Surrender, sir! surrender your ship, or overboard you go! Haul down your flag."

The Englishman was completely thrown aback, nor did he comprehend his situation till he saw the stars and stripes rise to the gaff of the schooner, and he knew then that he had been entrapped.

His crew were not prepared, their arms were stowed away, and it was madness to resist, therefore he had but one choice and that was to haul down his flag and submit.

Ballentine at once gave orders to secure his prisoners, for the crew of the transport was nearly as great as his own; and having done this, he asked the commander if he had letters or passengers.

"Both," was the reply; "a bag of the one you'll find below in my room, the only two of the other stands aft there on the poop."

Ballentine glanced in the direction signified by his prisoner, and as his eye settled upon the elder of the two, a look of recognition gathered in it, and stepping hastily towards him, he exclaimed,—

"Is it possible, sir, that I see *you* here? I thought you were in England, in peace and safety."

"You *do* see me here, *sir!*" responded the other; "when a son forgets the *duty* he owes to his parent and to the land of his nativity, it is time for a parent to forget peace and comfort and endeavour to reclaim him."

"If that be the sole cause of your visit, I regret that you have taken unnecessary trouble," replied the young commander, in a tone as cold and even more calm than that used by his father, for the other speaker was none other than Count Ballentine.

"Unnecessary!— you will not dare to persist in your *rebellion* when ——."

"Sir, call my present duty by a milder name, if you please, or I shall be forced to forget that you are my father and remember that you are my prisoner. I have chosen to serve, not England's rebellious colonies, but the free United States · and I will do so with my life!"

"Then, sir, if you persist in that choice, hear *me!* I will disinherit you—you shall neither have my title nor my gold."

"Father, it is well; I ask not your title nor your gold! But of this, my honour, my unsullied fame, the name of my ancestors, and the pure pride of my heart, you cannot strip me!"

The father seemed to feel his son's remarks, and for a moment appeared about to relent and change his tone, when a few whispered words from the one who stood beside him, Ricard, caused him to turn away without a softening word.

The son, sadly but calmly, also turned away, and in a very short time Mr Barnacle reported all ready for the vessels to part company, and then again young Ballentine approached his parent.

"Sir," said he, "it would pain me to send you in as an English prisoner, therefore I offer you a room in my cabin until I can land you in America."

"If you will return to your duty, and act as the son of a nobleman should, I will accept your offer," replied the elder.

"I am now doing that which I deem my duty as a man," replied the son; "and I await your answer. If you will only treat me as a son, my cabin is at your service." But you have your own choice, sir," said Ballentine, as he returned to his own deck.

In a few moments the vessels had separated, one bearing away to the southward, the other continuing her course, for a cruise.

CHAPTER VII.

"Foiled again, by Heaven! foiled again in an attempt to obtain an interview with 'that beautiful witch!'"

Thus cried Frank Dorsey, as he turned his horse's head away from the old mansion at

Helle-gat, where he had just been informed that Miss Katrine was not at home. Just as he had made this remark, in facing down a little ravine which opened toward the water, he saw the fluttering of a lady's dress amid the leafless trees, and as he reined in his horse saw that a female was walking by the water side. Her back was toward him, therefore he could not determine whether this was she whom he had been seeking, yet he thought he recognised the queenly step and graceful figure.

Therefore he quickly turned his horse into a little copse of thick-growing hazel, where he fastened him; then he stole cautiously down the ravine, toward the water side. A near approach to the female removed all doubts in his mind as to her identity—she was indeed Katrine Van Twiller, and, what seemed to him most auspicious, she was alone.

She seated herself upon the lowermost of a little ledge of rocks which jutted down from the hill into the water, near the spot where her lover had landed on the occasion of his last visit, and here she seemed to watch the rippling waves as they chased each other into the crevices of the rock, or dissolved in foam. She seemed sad, for ever and anon her lips would open to let a sigh escape, and her dark blue eyes seemed almost as liquid as the waves she gazed upon. Her situation was almost entirely secluded from the view of all surrounding points, the cliff behind her hid the house from her sight, and only from the water or from the narrow ravine which led to the spot could she be seen or approached.

Towards her, as thus she sat, stealthily crept Frank Dorsey, and he probably would have gained her side before she knew of his vicinity had he not disturbed a loose stone, which, tumbling down the rocks, gave her warning of an intruder.

Springing to her feet she glanced around, and as she saw him, her flashing eye and heightening colour betokened her displeasure. He gave her no time to express it in words, for quickly advancing, he said, in a gay, free tone,—

"Good morrow, fair lady! I visited your father's house to see you, but, not finding you at home, have taken the liberty of seeking you; and methinks this is a far more pleasant reception room than your parlour would be!"

"I should prefer the former, sir, when I am *forced* to receive visitors," replied the lady, in a cold, dignified tone; "but if Lieut. Dorsey will inform me what is his business, I will be obliged to him, for in my solitary rambles I am not fond of company."

Entirely disregarding the palpable hit, Dorsey answered,—

"Surely a fair lady need not ask a gallant cavalier what his business is, when he seeks her company!"

His manner was so respectful that Katrine paused and answered,—

"Well, sir, speak, and be brief."

"I came to avow my love—a love which, from the first hour that I looked upon you, has burned within my breast, and to offer you my hand—yes, to give you one of the proudest

———————————!" exclaimed the young officer, with passionate eagerness.

"I cannot accept either your love or your hand. Let this be your final answer!" responded Katrine, calmly but firmly.

Then came a change over the manner of the officer; he sprang to his feet, and, while his face grew red with mortification, and his dark eyes glared like living coals of fire, he cried,—

"You have rejected my honourable offer of love, Katrine Van Twiller; you've seen me bend my proud heart and kneel at your feet, and you have dared to scorn me—me, Frank Dorsey, who never was foiled before. But now beware! You have refused me, but I swear by all that's bright in heaven or dark in hell, that you shall be mine!"

"Stand back, sir, and let me return to my home," cried Katrine, her eyes flashing with indignation.

"Not till you answer me," replied Dorsey. "Do you know the commander of the 'Ocean Queen?'"

"If I do, I know him to be a man. I cannot say so much for you, sir! Stand back and give me the path."

"No, fair damsel, not yet; I have one word more to say. From your blushes as well as your language, I am led to believe that you have another lover, and that lover is the commander of the privateer. I shall first secure him—then beware for yourself. I am one who never yet was foiled in any aim, nor will I be now. By fair means or foul I will possess you. Had you responded to my love as you ought, but a few moments since, you might have been my wedded wife; now you shall be——"

He bent forward and whispered the rest; and deeply insulting must those words have been, for the maiden sprang toward him, and as he had bowed his face toward her, spat full upon it, crying at the same time—

"Begone, base hind—begone from my path!"

The eyes of Dorsey flashed fire at this insult, and then he seemed on the point of springing upon her, when the sound of a man whistling some odd air was heard, and the next moment our old friend, Hans Nipperhausen, was seen advancing along the ravine.

'Thank God! for this interruption," cried Katrine. "Now, sir, you will permit me to pass, I presume!" she added to Dorsey; but the latter, who seemed choked and maddened with anger, cried,—

"No; not were your whole _rood at your side!"

The maiden looked but once at Hans, who with short pipe between his teeth was slowly coming down the rocks, and then attempted to pass by Dorsey.

The latter stretched out his hand to prevent her, but as he did so, Hans, with one quick and lengthy leap, landed on the rock at his side, then quick as thought raised him in his powerful arms and pitched him from the rock into the water at its foot.

"Your fadder wants you, Miss Kate," said Hans, as he did this; and before the head of the maddened officer was above the water, the fair girl had turned to obey the request.

Hans, meantime, quietly seated himself upon the rock, and while he seemed to puff his pipe with increased pleasure, he watched the movements of the other.

Dorsey, when he arose to the surface of the water, which was at that season cold as ice, could scarcely speak, but spluttering and cursing, he swam back to the rock, upon which, in a moment, he landed. As soon as he got a foot-hold, he rushed up to the spot where Hans sat smoking, and drawing a pistol from his breast, shouted,—

"You shall die, you cursed dog—you shall die for this!"

He pulled the trigger, but no report followed, and Hans drew a heavier whiff as, without moving from his seat, he said,—

"De priming pe wet in de pan, captain. Dere's no use for powder when it is wet."

"No; curse you; but if this is wet it won't miss fire!" shouted Dorsey, as he attempted to draw his sword, but ere he could get it entirely from its scabbard, Hans was again by his side, and once more Mr Dorsey enjoyed a cold bath free. Losing his grasp upon his sword as he struck the water the second time, it sunk to the bottom, and he arose defenceless, so far as weapons were concerned.

Hans, after pitching him from the rocks, reseated himself and again commenced puffing his pipe, as calmly as if nothing had occurred to alter or disturb his usual equanimity.

Completely chop-fallen, and quite cooled off in body, was the lieutenant as he scrambled again up the cold and rugged rocks, but there was a raging hell within his breast.

He did not now approach the strong-armed old Dutchman, but with only one fiery glance of fiendish anger, passed on up the ravine.

In a few moments he reached his horse, which he mounted and rode toward the city. Bitter were his thoughts and threatening his soliloquy, as he rode on.

"By heaven! she and all who belong to her shall suffer for this!" he cried—"never before was I so thwarted, but she shall repent it. Before another week passes by, she shall be in my power, and that Dutch rascal shall die!"

CHAPTER VIII.

It was a few nights later than when we last saw her, that the "Ocean Queen" was steering down along the coast of Long Island, just to the northward of Sandy Hook.

At dusk on that evening she had weighed anchor, and slipped out from a little cove where she had been concealed for several days, refitting and preparing for active service.

Her crew seemed to be overjoyed on feeling once more the swell of the heaving ocean, and "piled" the canvas on her with a hearty good will, and soon she was dashing at a rapid rate through the water, leaving behind her a long wake of snowy foam.

Her commander and his first lieutenant, Mr Barnacle, who had just returned from leaving his prize at Norfolk, and Karl Van Twiller, were seated aft. by the taffrail, in conversation, and the men were grouped around forward, some engaged in spinning, others in listening to yarns.

Four or five old forecastle-men were seated upon the head-rail, listening to the oracle of their part of the vessel, old Tom Crossan, who had seen more service than any man on board, and who was acknowledged by all hands to be a regular out-and-out sailor, every inch of him.

Tom was about fifty years of age, had a very red face, his thin hair was long, black, and as curly as the long beard which hid his swarthy neck from view. He was full six feet four inches high, rather spare in form, but one of those who seem made up of bone and muscle, without any spare flesh upon them.

He was so strong, that once when the best bower of the schooner caught on the rail, when they were letting it go, he stepped up on the rail, raised the anchor with his hands and pitched it clear, though it did weigh nine hundred pounds.

Tom's chum, or nearest friend aboard, was a little, short half-breed Indian, who had shipped with him, and who it was said belonged to one of the tribes who still encamped about the waters of the Hudson river, loath to leave the hunting-grounds of their ancestors. When Camar, the Indian, first came aboard with "long Tom," as the crew always called Crossan, he knew but little about a sea-going vessel, but he was very apt, and soon was as handy on the flying-jib-boom, or in stowing a staysail, as any man aboard. He too, like "long Tom,", became a general favourite, for in action he had proved as cool and active as his chum, and the two were looked upon by their commander as the most valuable of all his crew.

"Do you see there, Cam," said Tom, as the Indian, with two or three others of the forecastle-men, bent over the bows; "do you see our lady's face—you can see it as the foam throws sparkles of light up into it. Don't you see she looks glad that we're out again on the deep water. Ever since we've been in that ere bloody cove, her eyes have been as green as ever a cat's was, and her face looked as if she was a grievin' for somethin'."

"So they did—I never seed such a figure-head afore! I do believe its bewitched?" responded one of the seamen.

"Bewitched!" continued Tom; "to be sure it is. I've never had no doubts about that since we came out of Cherbourg, for while we lay in that bloody French port, her eyes were green and her face as dirty lookin' as if never a drop of decent paint had ever been put upon her, but when we got off into clear water, I can tell you that she brightened up, like a sewing girl on a Sunday. Her eyes got as blue, and her face as cheerful as if she was a human, didn't it, Cam?"

"Yes, me see it. She be great medicine-woman!" replied the Indian, who always regarded and called the sorcerers of his tribe medicine-men.

"I do believe there's something been done

to bewitch that figure-head, for I remember the night when it was blowing so heavy, and we'd got close in on Hatteras shoals without know'n' it that I looked at her face when a flash of lightnin' lit it up; and her eyes were as green as ever I seen 'em! I went aft and told the skipper, and then he made me heave the lead as soon as I could, and there we were in only four fathom water.

"The witch know'd as well as could be that we was going ashore, and she was mad. We didn't but just have time to go about on t'other tack before the breakers were in sight. If it hadn't been for her eyes that night, the schooner and all hands would have gone to Davy Jones' locker."

The men looked at the figure-head, but said nothing. The whole crew seemed to think that it was bewitched, and that the schooner was safe so long as it was preserved.

They had repeatedly asked the captain about it, but he had always smiled mysteriously and evaded answering their question. This settled the matter in their minds, and in alluding to the figure-head, they always spoke of it very respectfully, terming it "*our lady.*"

While the crew were thus engaged, the officers aft were holding a conversation, the drift of which can only be inferred by giving it to the reader.

"I hate to trust the barkie in the bay again so soon, especially with a leading wind in; but I must be at Helle-gat cove before midnight," said Ballentine, to whom Barnacle responded.

"It's true that the bull-dogs will be apt to

keep a bright look-out after all that's past, but still I think we might get in and out again, as we did before."

"A pitcher that goes too often to the well is apt to get broken. I don't like to put 'our lady' into danger so great very often."

"Why must you go in?" asked Karl; "it seems to me that there's a better chance for both prize money and fair play out here than there is inside."

"I have an engagement to be at Helle-gat cove this night, and you know that I never break an engagement."

"Well, if you dislike to risk the schooner, why not go in with your boat?" suggested Barnacle.

"True, I can do so; and in the trip with her I can see if there isn't a chance for cutting out something. We have done so little lately, that I'm afraid we'll forget how to work when a chance comes."

"Light, ho! on the starboard bow, sir!" cried a lookout from forward.

"The glim on the highlands, I reckon," said Barnacle; "shall we luff in or will you take your boat?"

"I think the boat is best," said Ballentine; "I'll take only six men, beside myself."

"Who'll you have, sir?"

"Long Tom, little Cam, and four of my gigs-men, in the whale-boat. Have them all armed with pistols and cutlasses, and lay half-a-dozen muskets in the stern sheets of the boat."

"Aye, aye. sir. I must heave to and lower the boat to get you off."

"Certainly, Mr Barnacle, do so."

In a few moments the schooner lay with her topsail aback, and all was made ready to despatch the boat. This having been done, was reported to the commander, who stepping into her, bade the crew hoist her two lug sails, and taking the tiller into his own hand, headed her in over the bar, before a stiff breeze, which gave him a leading course up the bay.

Before he left the vessel he gave orders to Mr Barnacle to remain where he was until daylight, and if he did not return by that time to run back to Montauk point. In case he still missed him, to consider that he had fallen into the hands of the enemy and to act according his own judgment.

"Where do you think Captain Ballentine's father is now?" asked Karl of Mr Barnacle, a short time after the captain had left the schooner.

"I expect he's in New York before now," replied the other. "When I landed him at Norfolk, and told him he was free, and that by his son's orders, he swore that if he had any influence with Sir Henry Clinton, he would send the whole fleet out after us, and cursed his son for a rebel and everything else but a gentleman."

"I hope that he will have sense enough to stay where he is without coming into these latitudes to give us trouble," responded the other.

Reader, we will change to other scenes now, so look out for us in the next chapter.

CHAPTER IX.

When Count Ballentine and his servant were landed at Norfolk, and found that they were free, the first thoughts of the father who had recovered from his anger, was to return with Mr Barnacle to his son's vessel, for the latter told him that he should at once proceed overland to a certain point, which was agreed upon, to join the "Ocean Queen."

But to this the servant, who seemed to have a strange influence over his master, objected, insisting upon their going to New York and placing themselves under the protection of General Clinton.

To this Count B. acceded, and at the very moment when young Hunt Ballentine left his vessel to go into harbour on a visit to Katrine Van Twiller, his father had taken quarters at the old tavern fronting the South Ferry landing, having just arrived overland from Norfolk after a most fatiguing and dangerous journey.

One hour later and his son scudded past that very point, with a flowing sheet, as he steered toward Helle-gat cove.

And where was Katrine at this same hour? Let the following inform the reader:—

With the light upon her window ledge as before, she sat and gazed down toward the water. The wind whistled through the leafless trees, but it was to her a cheerful sound, for this was the night when *he*, her loved one, had promised to be by her side.

Looking around to the old clock which stood upon the mantelpiece, she murmured—

"Twelve o'clock and he not here yet?" Then a shadow of impatience crossed her fair brow and she looked out upon the water, and through the gloom she saw a light down by the water side, and her eye brightened as she said—

"That must be he—but no, Hans carries a lantern with him," and again she sighed, as if she feared a disappointment.

She still looked out, however, and as she did so, she thought that she saw the forms of two persons standing in the shadow of the trees below her.

Steadily she gazed upon them, until she felt satisfied that they were living beings, and then she wondered who they could be, or what their errand there at that hour. She knew that Ballentine was not one to stand and coldly watch the window of his mistress; she knew that Hans had gone to the waterside, and an undefinable dread of an unknown danger stole over her soul, as she gazed out from behind her half-drawn window curtains.

Hearing a step upon the stairs which led to her chamber, she turned with a frightened look, as if she expected peril was at hand, but her look changed as she met the fond look of her lover.

"Dear Hunt!" she cried, as she embraced him and returned his salutation, "have you sent any of your crew, as a watch, to the rear of the house?"

"No, dear Kate; what put that thought into your head?"

"I saw, but now, two persons lurking in the

shadow of the old oak, whose branches touch our walls. Who could they have been?"

"In the shadow of the oak—two persons lurking? I'll see," cried the lover, as he hastened to the window and looked out.

"I see no one, Kate," said he; and then, when she too looked forth, she found that they were gone.

"It is strange—I saw them very plain," said she, as her lover suggested that she had mistaken shadows of the branches for men, but he soon made her forget the circumstance as he related to her his escape.

Then she too told him of her adventures, and gay was his laugh, as he listened to the manner in which Hans had cooled the passion of the English lieutenant; yet even with his laugh came a shadow of care across his face as he thought of the exposed situation of his love, and he remarked—

"This man's name is Dorsey—a lieutenant aboard the 'Harpy,' you say, Kate?"

"Yes, Hunt; so he told me, and I rated him for being ashore when he had enemies afloat."

"Well, I'll soon take care of him. If he be aboard of his craft to-morrow night, I'll give him a chance to make love to me."

"How?—what dare-devil freak have you in your mind?"

"Only to cut out that same 'Harpy' at this hour, or a little later, to-morrow night She is too smart a vessel to belong to the English. I want to either take or destroy her, and being, as you know, rather wilful, shall do it!"

"It is too dangerous, dear Hunt; she is in the harbour, in the very midst of the fleet."

"She won't be there long," replied the other; "but let us talk of other things. I've only half-an-hour to spend here to-night, for I don't want to be seen this time."

When the fair Katrine thought she saw two persons beneath her window, she was not mistaken. One of them was Frank Dorsey, the other was Lieutenant Walcott, the red-faced *spongy* individual whom we introduced in a former chapter to the reader.

The business of Dorsey was a tour of inspection around the old mansion, preparatory to another visit, with a most foul and base intent.

When they first saw the light in the maid's window, Walcott whispered,—

"This must be the girl's room: old Dutchmen don't sit up so late as this."

"Yes, it is her room," replied Dorsey, "and it seems to me that it's right handy to get at, for the limbs of this old oak tree rub against the wall of the house. I'm sure I could easily get in."

"Aye, that's true; but how would you get her out?" responded the other.

"Gag her—tie her and then lower her down by a rope. Then it's but a step to the water: have a boat's crew there, and it would be an easy job to get her aboard the 'Harpy.'"

"Won't old McKannon make a fuss about it? Will he let you bring a woman aboard?"

"I gave him a hundred pounds last night for the free use of the cabin, hinting to him what I wanted it for, and he took the money. You know he loves money more than you do grog."

"Then he must have a liking for it," responded the other. "By the way, Frank, have you not a pistol with you?"

The younger villain drew a small liquor flask from his pocket and handed it to the other.

After taking a long draught from it, he looked up again at the window and said,—

"That's the gal's room—ah, by thunder! there she is herself!"

"Yes, it is her!" said Frank Dorsey, as he gazed, with a passionate eye upon her, "and she looks this way, but it is too dark for her to discover us; yet we will go."

At that moment a step was heard approaching, a heavy, staggering step, and Dorsey, bidding his companion keep close, crouched down closer by the trunk of the tree. As he did this he thought he saw the form of a man pass noiselessly by, in the path which led from the water to the house, but, as a moment after, the light of a lantern borne by Hans Nipperhausen, whose step he had heard, came gleaming along the path, he thought he had only seen a shadow of the tree.

"Where the devil can that fellow have been at this time of night, I wonder?" muttered he, and when he saw that the Dutchman had a lobster net over his shoulder, he seemed more satisfied, supposing that the man had been taking up his net at the low tide, which was at that hour.

Hans passed on, not seeing the two spies,

and they soon hurried away toward the city, little dreaming how near they had been that night to the dreaded commander of the "Ocean Queen."

Early on the next morning, before the rosy dawn had tinted the eastern sky, Captain Ballentine had regained his vessel, which stood away to the northward, close in shore, to avoid being seen by the English cruisers.

"I've found work for us to-night, Barnacle," cried the young captain, as he saw his vessel draw away, after getting on board.

"What is it, sir—more cutting out?"

"You are a capital hand at guessing. It is just that, and nothing else. I have taken the bearings of that schooner, the 'Harpy,' and I intend to pay my respects to her captain to-morrow night."

"Isn't she in a bad place for us?"

"There are four or five other crafts not far from her, but she lays outside, and if the wind tends out of the bay, I think we can get her. She won't expect an attack, and the taking of her may not cost a man."

"Too good luck to expect, that would be, sir," responded the first luff; "but I hope it'll come true, that's all."

"If it should not, our brave men will never flinch from it. I do believe I could have taken her to-night with my boat's crew, if I had time, for I went close under her bows and never was even hailed."

"They mistook you for one of their own boats, I suppose," said Barnacle: "but I'll go forward and set the men to getting the arms and boats ready for service."

"Do so; we shall run down to the bar as soon as it gets dark, and then let them look out for squalls."

CHAPTER X.

IT was night, the hour not later than ten, and yet Katrine Van Twiller was about retiring to her couch, for on the previous night she had remained up very late with her lover, and even when he had returned to his vessel she had been sleepless, for she knew how dangerous was his passage through the bay.

Her father, who, like the steady-habited people of his race, kept early hours, both at night and in the morning, had already retired to his couch, and was probably at this moment snoring like an over-fed Indian. Even old Hans Nipperhausen had crept into his comfortable bed, and everything living about the old mansion seemed at rest, except the fair Katrine. No, not everything, for Katrine, as she began to prepare to retire, heard the old watch-dog bark loudly, but she thought nothing of that, for the faithful animal would bark at night, if he heard but the galloping of a horse on the distant road. Besides, she knew that her father's doors were heavy and well barred, and that Hans slept in the porter's room inside of them, and she had no fear of intruders.

Poor girl! how little dreamed she of the danger near her at that very moment. The dog had suddenly ceased barking, and was entirely still, and she thought no more of his warning.

One look with us, reader, to a scene that is passing in the vicinity. At the moment when Katrine heard the barking of the dog, a boat, manned by six seamen, with two persons sitting in her stern sheets, landed at the rock in the cove where Dorsey received his ducking at the hand of old Hans. The dog had discovered them, and commenced barking as he saw the two who were in the stern-sheets advance up the hill toward the house.

"Curse that dog! he will wake everybody within a mile!" muttered the younger of the two, who was closely wrapped in a boat-cloak.

"Just hold on a bit, old fellow, and I'll clap a stopper on him!" replied the other, at the same time advancing to the spot where the dog had paused on the edge of the rock. The dog growled as the man advanced, but the latter drew a short hanger, which he wore at his side, and with a quick blow cut through the entire neck-bone of the animal, which, without another growl, sunk dead upon the ground.

"Very neatly done, Walcott; upon my word you'd make a capital dog-killer for the corporation,' said the other, in a low tone; then looking toward the window, he added, "see, *she* is up yet; we had better wait an hour."

"Why so, Frank?—the rest of the house is still. It's late now, and we'll have little time enough to get her safe aboard before daylight."

"True," answered the other, "have you the rope-ladder with you?"

"Aye—I've forgotten nothing, not even a bosom companion, a soul-comforter," replied the other, first showing a bundle of rope coiled up, and then drawing from his breast pocket a small bottle which, uncorking, he placed to his lips. From a low, gurgling sound which murmured pleasantly from his throat, as a little brook when it runs over a pebbly bottom, it was easy to infer that the bottle was not empty. After a long pull at the same, the drinker spoke to his companion—

"Try some, Frank; it's real old Jamaica, and will give you spunk for the business."

"I'd drink," replied the other, "not to gain spunk for carrying her off, but because it is so infernal chilly to-night."

To do this, the speaker paused under the branches of the tree which stood so close to the window of Katrine. Having drank, he returned the bottle to his companion, who again putting it to his lips, held it there until it would yield no more liquid to his lips.

"Now hold on below and keep a bright look-out, while I go up and fasten the rigging," said the younger man, "and when I'm ready, come up half way, so as to take her as I pass her out."

At the same time ascending the tree by the opposite side from the window, and in the shade. The ascent was easy, for it was a thick-branched tree.

When we were last speaking of Katrine, she had noticed that the dog no longer barked, and supposing all to be quiet and safe, she began to prepare to retire to her bed; but first she knelt down and offered up her pure prayers to the Throne of Grace, and well we know that her lover's name was mentioned then.

And even at this moment a pair of wicked eyes, the hateful fire were bent upon her, and even her occupation could not affect him who gazed upon her. He saw that her back was turned toward him as she knelt, and stealthily crept along the limb to the window ledge and gently tried the casement. It was unfastened, and he found that it could be raised.

Beckoning his companion up to his assistance, the intruder prepared to raise the window. This he did just at the moment when the lovely girl was arising from her knees, and she turned toward him at the moment he raised the sash and sprang in to the chamber.

She screamed in terror as she recognised the features of Dorsey, and that long, shrill cry of fear echoed through the house, like the cry of some bird frightened from its nest. She had no time to fly, no time to scream again; in one instant she was seized in the villain's arms, wrapped closely in his cloak, and though she struggled wildly, was passed out of the window and down the ladder, by the aid of Walcott, Dorsey's vile confederate.

"Be quick—be quick!" cried the latter, as he saw lights flashing through the house, "that screech of her's has raised all hands."

"All safe," said Dorsey, as he reached the ground; "stay and get the ladder, Walcott."

"No time for that, run for the boat!"

shouted the other, as a form was seen to darken the window, and then a voice shouted from above, "Sthop dere you tam divils—sthop, or I'll shoot!" which was followed by the report of a blunderbuss, which scattered its shot in such close proximity to the red-faced lieutenant, that he tumbled over the edge of the cliff and down the rocks, as if he had been shot, though indeed he was untouched.

Dorsey, bearing his helpless victim, rushed down the path and was in a moment at the boat, which already contained his companions.

"Shove off, boys!—shove off quick, or we'll have all Holland down after us!" cried Dorsey, as he sprang into the boat, and even while the men were doing so, they heard the footsteps of Hans, who, descending by the window and rope ladder, was close upon them.

But yet he was too late, the boat was clear of the strand, and in it he saw the struggling but helpless form of his mistress.

"Sthop der poat!" he shouted; "sthop der poat and pring my mistress pack again and I giff one tousan tollar!"

"Stop your noise, you old fool!" shouted Dorsey; "tell your master that Miss Katrine is off on a pleasure cruise with a lieutenant of the Royal Navy—going to sea in his yacht, d'ye hear?"

"Oh mine Got! oh mine Got!" cried the unhappy Hans, "sthop der boat."

But it was in vain he cried, the boat was now dashing down the East River with all the speed which six bending oars could give to it. Meantime the house at the cove was all alarmed. The father of Katrine, aroused first by her shriek and then by the report of Hans' gun, had rushed to her chamber, where finding that she was gone he rushed out, not by the way taken by his faithful servant, but by the regular door, following Hans, whom he knew by his shouting. He arrived at the moment when the lieutenant shouted the message for himself, and he groaned in the agony of his heart as he saw the boat dash off into the night-gloom and felt that he could not rescue his unhappy child.

"What shall we do—what shall we do to save my child from that lawless villain's grasp?" groaned the miserable father, and his groan was echoed by the faithful Hans. The latter now turned toward the house with hasty steps, not knowing what to do, yet wishing to do something, when suddenly he stumbled over the body of the dog.

"Tam! I dink I haf shoot one!" he cried, as he kicked at the body; "yes, he is here, py tam!" cried Hans, with a more joyful tone. He thought that he had killed one of them, and this gave him some pleasure.

But his joy was as quickly dispelled, when some of the domestics who had just been aroused, rushed down the hill-side with a lantern and he found out his mistake.

"Dog!—throat cut! my pullets didn't do that!" he muttered, as he turned over the poor animal.

"No, this has been a regular planned affair," moaned the father. "I see it all—that villain got mad at Kate fer writing a refusal to his request, and now he has carried her off. Oh God! she is in his power—she is lost for ever!"

"No, py tam!" cried the honest Hans; "no, py tam she shall not be lost! I'll go to der gobernor—I'll tell him all der dam rascality."

"Yes," cried the father, the thought of the governor striking him as an only hope, "jump on the grey colt and ride at full speed to Sir Henry Clinton's quarters. Tell him of this foul outrage, and that I demand justice and that right speedily. Tell him which way the boat is gone, and pray him to have her stopped. Use every means—I will give ten thousand dollars for her safe return."

Hans waited not to answer; with the first thought he had bounded toward the stable and within two minutes more he was riding at a break-neck speed toward the city. He had not even time to saddle the animal or to bridle it, he guided it with its heavy rope halter, using the loose end for a whip. He made such "time" over that road, too, on that night, as many a blooded nag might be proud of, though the dam of the colt was nothing but an old plough horse.

And while he was thus speeding to the city by land, Dorsey's boat was darting in the same direction over the water.

It was not quite twelve when Hans stopped his colt before the quarters of Sir Henry Clinton, and at the very same moment Dorsey arrived in sight of his vessel.

"Give way, lads, we'll soon be aboard," he

cried to the men. At this moment Walcott touched him on the shoulder and said, as he pointed toward the schooner—

"There's other boats on the water to-night besides ours. Let's see—one, two — four. Yes, four boats, and they row towards the schooner."

"Give way lively, boys, it must be some cutting-out party. Give way—I'm ruined if I'm not aboard," cried Dorsey.

At this moment he heard the shout of the sentinel on board the "Harpy," as he hailed the boats, and then no answer being returned, he saw the flash of the soldier's musket, and saw the boats dash in toward the vessel.

"Too late, by thunder! too late," he shouted; and then, as if in hopes to aid his vessel, he cried again, "Give way, men, we must go alongside."

"It's no use—you can't do any good now. You may thank your stars you're not aboard," said Walcott, evidently better satisfied where he was, than with the prospect of the hard knocks which he might have gotten gratis just at that moment on board of the schooner.

CHAPTER XI.

LONG before the sun went down on the day which closes our ninth chapter, the crew of the "Ocean Queen" were prepared for the expedition to cut out the "Harpy." For reasons best known to himself, Ballentine had stood off the coast until the land was entirely out of sight, and the water was as blue as his own

Katrine's eye. The crew were in fine spirits, for Long Tom had made a particular examination of the "magical lady," who served their vessel for a figure-head, and pronounced her favourable to their designs.

"Her eye," he said, "was blue as a bit of the Gulf Stream, and as clear as a cloudless sky;" and then he swore that he saw her smile as he stood on the bowsprit, holding on by the foretopmast stay, gazing wistfully to know whether luck would attend them on the proposed expedition.

Tom, and Cam, the Indian, were to go in the captain's own boat, and both seemed more than usually pleased with the idea. The men had been engaged all day with their arms—grinding their cutlasses and battle-axes, and cleaning the locks of their pistols.

Spare oars were placed in each boat, and those used were neatly muffled. Before the sun went down, Ballentine, having mustered his crew at quarters and closely inspected them, gave orders to tack the schooner and stand in for the land. Having kept the bearings of the latter, he gave his helmsman a compass course which he knew would take him near Sandy Hook, and as the night came on, crowded on the canvas and hurried his little craft in toward the point of her destination.

He had overheard Long Tom giving the crew the cheering news in regard to the favourable looks of the figure-head, and felt quite sure that this, in their superstitious minds, would have a great effect, and a most beneficial one, yet he smiled, as if the change in her looks on that day was no secret to him.

It was near ten o'clock before the schooner gained a position near the mouth of the little swash channel, just to the northward of the main bar, from which Ballentine intended to start with his boats. These were soon lowered, the schooner having been hove to, with her head off shore, and the picked crews were not long in taking their places in them. They were forty in number, men who had been oft tried in scenes like that which they expected on that night. This left twenty men to manage the vessel, which Ballentine left under the charge of his boatswain, a staunch and trusty old seaman, with directions to stand off and on, with short tacks, and to keep a bright look for signals from him. Should he prove successful, as soon as he got the "Harpy" in his hands he was to send up a rocket which could easily be seen from the outside, but if he failed the rocket would not be shown, and the privateer was to keep close in to the bar, to be ready to receive or aid the boats.

First giving a second look to the men in each boat, and seeing that they were perfectly fitted for service, Ballentine gave the order to shove off, taking the lead in his own boat and steering in by the beacon light on the Highlands of Never-sink.

Next to his boat followed that commanded by Barnacle, and next to that came Karl. The rear boat was commanded by the gunner, an old fellow who had lost one eye from the thrust of a boarding pike, when they cut out the "Fire-fly" some months previous, and now begged for only a chance to revenge the loss and perform a similar favour for some Englishman.

With muffled oars, and a long, steady pull, the boats swept in over the bar, and keeping close up along the starboard shore, steered for the cluster of lights which, in the Narrows ahead of them, pointed out the place where the English fleet was at anchor.

When they got within about a mile of these, the head boat lay upon its oars, and the others closed up to receive their final orders.

"Which is her light?" asked Barnacle, as he gazed at the cluster.

"The one nearest to us, most to the south'ard!" replied the young captain. "You can see that it is lower than the rest, as she is the smallest craft there. I took her bearings carefully."

"Then we've so much the better chance to get her out after she is taken. Wind and tide both in our favour—she's ours sure as a gun."

"Yes," replied the commander; "I've no fear on that score, and now we'll arrange how to board her. You will board on the bow, followed by the gunner and his crew, Mr Barnacle. I will take the waist, and Karl shall go in over the taffrail. She won't have many men on deck, and the minute you are aboard, men, spring to the hatchways and keep the crew from gaining the deck."

These orders were given so that each man might know his duty, and now the boats again started toward the light which had been pointed out as the "Harpy's," keeping to the southward of the other lights and pulling carefully but steadily along.

The night had been wearing on, and it was now midnight. The cries of the sentinels as they gave the usual "all's well" was heard, and old Linstock the gunner grinned horribly a ghastly smile, as he heard them, muttering in a low tone—

"You'll spin a different yarn before you're an hour older, you bloody sharks."

The boats were now closing up with the schooner rapidly, not more than a hundred yards off, when they knew that they were discovered, for her sentinel shouted—

"Boats, ahoy!"

Ballentine gave them no answer, but cried to his men—"Away there, lads! give way and board!"

Then came the discharge of the sentinel's musket and the sound of his cry as he shouted—"All hands, ho! The enemy are boarding us!"

The next moment the Americans were on the schooner's deck, where some ten or twelve of the crew had sprung half-naked from their berths, and now tried to resist, but in a moment they were mastered, some of them cut down, the rest disarmed. Obeying their leader's directions, the men had guarded the hatches, and only a few of the schooner's crew had gained the deck. The rest were safely caged below.

Karl had sprung to the cabin with his men, and reached it just in time to secure the officers, only three in number, who were rushing on deck, sword in hand. The old gunner did not have his wish, and no Englishman fell a victim on that night to his intention of having "an eye for an eye."

But all of this had not been done without giving alarm to the squadron. Lights could be seen glancing about from the other vessels, alarm guns were fired, and everything was in an uproar.

"Cut the cable!" shouted Ballentine, the moment he saw capture secured; "lay aloft a dozen of you and loose away the topsail and top-gallan' sail, man the sheets and halliards here on deck. Bear a hand!"

This was done rapidly, and then as he saw she was under motion, he cried to Karl to take the helm and steer her out for the bar. At this moment a ship near to them sent up a signal rocket, which illuminated the water far and near.

"Saved me the trouble—made my own signal," cried Ballentine, with glee, little seeming to care for the fact that this light had shown his position to the enemy.

"What's that? By thunder, we'd have had more prisoners if we'd waited a minute or two," said Barnacle, pointing to a boat which was laying on its oars, just astern of them, and had evidently been pulled toward the schooner. As Ballentine glanced toward it, he saw by the bright light of the rocket what he thought to be a female form struggling in the grasp of a man, and then as the light went out, he heard distinctly a stifled scream.

"By Heavens, there's some foul work going on there!" he cried; "but we've no time to see into it now."

Little did he dream from whose lips came that stifled shriek, or whose hand held the struggling form which he had seen.

The rocket had shown to the English the result of the attack and the position of the captured schooner, and now they opened a hot cannonade, which threw the shot thick and fast around her. But the "Harpy" was under sail; the wind was fresh, and a strong ebb-tide with her, so that she swiftly sped from them. It was not long before the prize was dashing out through the swash channel, and as he gained its mouth Ballentine sent up a rocket as a signal to his own vessel. The latter at once showed her position by a blue light, and the "Harpy" was soon within hail of her.

"Crowd on your canvas and follow me!" cried Ballentine, hailing the boatswain.

Mustering the captured crews, Ballentine became aware of the absence of two officers, and learned to his dismay that they were absent on a "lark"—after a Dutch girl named Katrine.

When Dorsey heard the exclamations of Katrine to her brother and lover—for she instinctively felt that the capturers of the "Harpy" could be no others—he instantly ordered the men to back water, then to turn the boat's head to the city and row thither.

Arrived there, Katrine was enveloped in a heavy boat-cloak and hurried to the "Swan" tavern, kept by an old wretch named Dunderhead. A bargain was quickly struck, and Katrine hastily carried into a stone addition to the tavern.

Soon after an orderly arrived at the house and summoned Dorsey before Sir Henry Clinton. The governor informed him that a complaint had been made that on the previous night Dorsey had carried off the daughter of a Dutch gentleman, from near Helle-gat. This Dorsey stoutly denied, and Sir Henry took his word for the time—being too busy to investigate the matter.

Scarcely had this matter been arranged when old Van Twiller made his appearance. He stood up stoutly before the governor, and detailed the abduction of his daughter, adding that he had himself seen Lieutenant Dorsey carrying her off. The governor was astonished, but promised the father redress.

This interview was cut short by the announcement that Count Ballentine was without. He was an old friend of Sir Henry Clinton, and after the first greetings had passed he recounted how he had been captured by the "Ocean Queen," and that the redoubtable commander of that famous craft was his son and heir.

While all these incidents were rapidly occurring, a whale-boat had skirted along the Brooklyn shore, passed Governor's Island, and was sailing into the city wharves. They were part of the crew of the "Ocean Queen."

"A good run we've made of it, Cam," said Tom, in a congratulatory tone; "a first-rate run, and, if we don't change our luck, we'll get in half-an-hour more."

"Yes; but"—and the Indian shook his head sadly as he spoke—"'em look lady in her face before we start and she look bad—eyes green, face like mud."

"Always so when we don't take her to sea," responded Tom.

"Wasn't the 'Harpy' a bit of good luck?" growled one of the hands forward.

"Yes; but we're sure to lose her. Don't believe we'll ever get a Continental shinplaster of prize money from her. But, hallo! what's that?"

This last exclamation of Tom's was caused by hearing a low cry, something that seemed between a moan and a shriek, which appeared to come from the end of a pier which he was just passing.

"Me see sumt'h white—like ghost!" said Cam, whose quick eye caught a sight of a figure, either sitting or lying on the end of the pier.

As the boat arrived opposite to the pier, the figure which Cam had seen was observed to move, and a feeble voice came like a painful sigh across the water,—

"Help—help, if ye are men. Oh, save me!"

These words fell on the ears of those in the boat, and Tom, regardless of all danger of discovery from shore, cried to his crew, "Lower down the sails there, for'ard—out oars. By the holy Moses, that's a woman's voice, and she's in distress!"

In an instant the boat was alongside the pier.

CHAPTER XII.

It was just at the grey of twilight that five men could be seen strolling carelessly up the road toward Mynheer Van Twiller's residence. We need scarcely say that they were the men sent by Dorsey to waylay poor Hans.

Upon arriving in sight of the house, the coxswain halted his men and turned a little aside into the hazel thicket which bordered the road.

"Hold on here, boys," said he, after placing them, "while I take a cruise up to windward and see how the land lays."

The men obeyed, and the coxswain, who was apparently pretty near sober, walked cautiously toward the house. He had not been gone over eight or ten minutes, when he came hurrying back, his face expressive of anything but pleasure.

"Be ready, lads," he cried, "be ready; we have got three instead of one to deal with; but we may as well make sure of *the* one whom the lieutenant told us to take care of. Mark him, he's the biggest; and if they don't all stop when I say the word, why, just pop away at him."

The sound of horses' hoofs advancing down the rocky road could now be heard. As these came near, the coxswain levelled his pistol and shouted,—

"Heave to, there, you bloody lubbers!—heave to, or I'll give you a broadside."

"Who the devil are you, and what do you want?" cried the foremost of them.

"You've got a Dutchman in convoy. I want to have a bit of a yarn with him, so just let him come along with us, and you and your friend may go to the devil."

"Py tam!" cried Hans, "py tam, dey is de same gang which peat me so in der morning."

"Ha! say you so?" cried Ballentine, who was the first speaker; "then this is some new plan of the villains. Upon them, Karl—come on Hans, don't hesitate," and the speaker drew a long rapier from its scabbard at his side, and dashed his spurs deep into the horse's flank. The animal sprang forward toward the seamen, whose leader now shouted,—

"Pick out the Dutchman in the middle—let him have it and then scatter!" As he said this he discharged his pistol, which was followed by a general discharge from all his men; but the coxswain never again gave an order. The rapier of Ballentine passed completely through and through his body as he turned to seek shelter in the thicket. As he fell to the earth with a heavy groan, that groan was echoed by the unfortunate Hans, who had been the sole object of the seamen's fire, and whose horse now galloped down the road without a rider.

Ballentine returned and sprang from his horse. While he knelt down by the side of the unfortunate Hans to examine his hurt, he bade Karl guard against a surprise from any of the gang who might return.

"Are you much hurt?" he asked, as he grasped the hand of poor Hans.

The poor fellow only answered with a feeble groan; and Ballentine felt the warm blood streaming out upon his hand as he placed it against his breast.

"Yes, I fear he is badly. Karl, we must take him back to the house and get surgical aid. This has been a foul deed. Lead your horse here—we must try and raise him to its back and then we can both support him in the saddle."

As Karl obeyed and led his horse up, Ballentine saw that the wounded man was trying to speak, and he bent down his head to catch his words.

"To Sir Henry—to der gobernor!" whispered the wounded man. "I must go—he tell me to come. To der gobernor's!"

"It is dangerous for us to go in that vicinity, yet if, as I fear, Hans is dying, we had better bear him there, and let Sir Henry know how this foul murder has been done."

"Is der oder one tead?" murmured Hans, alluding to the coxswain.

"Cold—dead as a stone," said Karl, who had been examining the body.

"Py tam put I pe glad!" murmured Hans, "for it was his pullet that is id my preast!" and even the pain of his wounds seemed somewhat to be forgotten by Hans in the thought that he was revenged.

Ballentine had some skill in wounds, and was not long in finding where Hans was hurt, and soon succeeded in partially stopping the flow of blood, but he saw no hope of saving the poor fellow's life.

With the aid of Karl, the man was placed upon one of the horses, and Karl seated behind him to steady him. They rode as fast as possible, for both knew that if there was any hope of saving Hans it would be in giving him speedy surgical aid.

They paused, however, for a moment, in the suburbs of the city, to look at what appeared to be the body of a man stretched out in the road.

"What? more murder!" cried Ballentine, as his eye met this form.

As he spoke the man stirred and half arose, at the same time muttered,—

"I'm all right as a brick, coxswain, all right and tight. I say, hallo! what the devil are you doing a-horseback?"

"This must be one of the party," said Karl. "He is drunk, and perhaps we can gain some information of him. I will question him. Say, fellow. why didn't you keep up with the party?"

"I did—I went ahead of 'em; but they kept a-going round and round all the time, so wouldn't wait for 'em. But I say, shipmate, what's that you've got afore you?"

"A drunken friend of mine." replied Karl. Won't you take a ride back to town with my friend—your party have all gone back?"

"Did they catch the Dutchman?" asked the sailor, who seemed yet stupefied with liquor.

"Oh, yes; that's all right. Your lieutenant wanted him stopped, didn't he?"

"Who told you that?" said the sailor; and then added,—

"If the rest of the boys have gone back I'll go too; so if your comrade there'll do as much for me as you have done for your friend, why, I'll take the chance and get aboard of his long-legged craft."

This was the very thing which Ballentine and Karl wanted, for they needed such a witness; and soon the sailor was mounted before Ballentine, and the party resumed their route into the city.

There we shall meet them in the next chapter, amid strange and stirring scenes.

CHAPTER XIII.

It was the hour of eight. The night, the same eventful one which closed our last chapter. Sir Henry Clinton and Count Ballentine were still together, conversing of the "good auld lang syne." But at this moment, while the iron tongue of the old town clock was telling the hour, one of the governor's orderlies entered and interrupted the conversation.

"An officer is below in the ante-room to see your lordship."

"An officer?" asked Sir Henry; and then he added, "Ah, yes, I remember. I had an engagement at this hour—I have an examination to make. Come down with me, Count; you know much of human nature, and may aid my judgment."

"I will attend you, Sir Henry," replied the Count, and both at once arose and repaired to the ante-room.

Upon entering, Sir Henry bowed coldly to the young officer who stood before him, and remarked:

"I am glad to see you so punctual, Mr Dorsey."

"*Dorsey!*" muttered the Count, as he partly turned away to hide his confusion. "This, then, is he; but he will not know me!"

The Count was mistaken. Dorsey knew him the moment he entered, but with singular coolness forced down all appearance of confusion, and without apparently a glance at him, replied to Sir Henry.

"It is ever my custom to be punctual, your Excellency, and it should be especially so now, when my honour and veracity are attacked."

"Right, sir; very right. But your accusers seem laggard."

"Perhaps, your lordship, they fear detection, and prefer not to meet one whom they have slandered," said the wily villain.

At this moment an orderly entered and reported that Mynheer Dietrich Van Twiller was in waiting to see the governor.

The cheek of the young officer paled as **he**

heard Sir Henry give the order to admit him, and this confusion was in a moment noted by the governor, who said sternly,—

"Now, sir, we will have this matter settled."

The next moment the father of Katrine entered, his face pale and haggard, his eyes sunken, his whole appearance indicative of the agony of his heart.

"I am here, Sir Henry," said he; "here after searching in vain for my unhappy child. But before me I see one who knows where she is—I demand that he be forced to produce her."

"Lieutenant Dorsey denies having seen her—denies having been within forty miles of your mansion at the hour when you say your daughter was torn from her home."

"He knows that he speaks falsely before God. Not only I but my trusty Hans are witnesses against him. I heard his scornful laugh as his boat dashed out into the stream, while my poor child was struggling in his arms. There were six oarsmen and one officer beside himself. How would I have known this had I not seen them?"

"True. That is a point which needs explanation on your part, sir," said Sir Henry to Dorsey.

But at this moment the orderly entered again and handed a paper to him.

The latter read it, and then turning to the occupants of the room, he said,—

"You must excuse me for a moment, gentlemen; I will return and continue this investigation."

In half-an-hour Sir Henry returned to the room.

"We will now proceed to carry out this examination," he said, as again he seated himself at his table. "Where are your men, Mr Dorsey—where is your favourite officer, Lieutenant Walcott?"

"My men, sir, are scattered around the town, probably at some drinking houses; Lieutenant Walcott can be found at the 'Swan' hotel, where he has taken quarters for the time."

"Very well, sir, we shall see. I have sent for your coxswain; meantime I have another witness on the opposite side!"

As the governor said this he stamped thrice upon the floor, and at the signal the door was thrown open, and two soldiers entered, bearing the ghastly form of poor Hans.

When Dorsey saw him his cheek grew more pale than ever—he knew that his plans had partly miscarried, and he knew not how far the governor had discovered them.

The governor saw that Dorsey was agitated, and in a stern tone cried,

"Now, sir, will you deny that yon dying man has been thus maltreated by your orders?"

"My orders?" echoed Dorsey, still determined to save himself, if possible; "surely, general, you jest with me!"

"Sir, this is no jesting matter. I see that you will force more proof. Soldiers, bring in that drunken sailor."

A moment had not elapsed ere the soldi

whom Ballentine had brought to town was led into the room.

"Fellow," cried Sir Henry, "tell me the truth, on the peril of your life. Where were you sent this evening when you started out of town?"

The sailor glanced at Sir Henry; he knew his rank, and trembled as he replied,—

"The coxswain told us, your honour, that we were bound up the road to cut out that bloody Dutchman, who has got his grave ticket ready, yonder."

"Who gave the orders?"

"The coxswain said Lieutenant Dorsey did, your honour," replied the man, now considerably sobered.

"Sir Henry, I protest against any such evidence. He is drunk," cried Dorsey.

"Pe I trunk, you tam tivil?" faintly cried Hans. And then he added, "Py tam, gubernor, I'm kilt, put I will not die till Miss Katrine is safe, so help me, mine Got!"

"Be calm my good fellow," replied Sir Henry; "be calm—all shall be done to save you!"

In the meantime Mynheer Van Twiller had rushed to his honest servant's side, and, turning to Dorsey, he shouted,—

"Is this another of your cursed works. Oh, villain! where is my daughter?"

"Yes, where is she?" added the general. "I am now satisfied of your guilt; your attempts to hide it are in vain."

"Let him find her!" replied the detected villain. "I have said I know nothing about her; if my word is not believed, then let the disbelievers better themselves!"

"Consider yourself arrested!" cried the governor. "I will have you court-martialled; aye, sir, and the most extreme punishment shall be inflicted upon you."

The father of Katrine now advanced, and begged, in the most heart-touching terms, that Dorsey would say where his poor daughter could be found.

"What can be done—what can be done for my poor girl?" cried the distracted father.

"I know not what can be done for *her*, but for him I have close guard and a speedy trial. Soldiers, lay down that wounded man and take this officer under guard," cried the governor.

"Can I not visit my quarters and be there under guard?" asked Dorsey, still preserving his forced calmness.

The governor was about to deny the request when the father of Katrine stepped forward and whispered a word in his ear. This seemed to change his mind, for he said,—

"Yes, sir; you may go to your hotel, but you will remain under charge of this guard."

The villain bowed and left the apartment.

CHAPTER XIV.

THE moment after Dorsey left the ante-room at General Clinton's quarters, the general ordered an officer whom he could safely trust to follow his every motion, and to report the least look or sign that might lead to the discovery of the unhappy Katrine.

Finding that Hans still lived, the surgeon advised that he should be removed to more comfortable quarters, and his master at once requested that he should be carried to the "Swan" hotel. This was done, and soon the landlord, Nicholas Dunderhead, was called upon to find a room for the poor fellow.

"What ish der matter, Hans?" said he, when he saw how badly his poor friend had been injured.

"Te tam English haf kilt me, dat ish all!" said Hans, feebly.

"Kilt you! for why?" asked mine host of the "Swan."

"All apout Miss Katrine, dat dey stole last night from der haus up at Helle-gat."

"Miss Katrine!" echoed Dunderhead; "Mynheer Van Twiller's tochter?"

"Yaas; and he will give ten tousand tollar to find her."

"Ten tousand tollar! — Mynheer Van Twiller's tochter! Py tam, maype it pe her in de pack room!" said the old man, in low tones to himself.

Hans, feeble as he was, had noticed that sparkle in the old man's eyes, and he seemed to *feel* that Dunderhead knew something of her whereabouts. Calling him closer, he said, —

"Nicholas, if you knows where der gal ish, for der sake of der holy Got tell me before I die! You shall haf der ten tousand tollar."

"Where is Mynheer Van Twiller?" asked the other.

"At der governor's. Shall I tell der soldier to go pring him here?" asked Hans.

"Yaas," muttered the old man; "yaas—ten tousand tollar—yaas!"

Hans waited not for more, he bade the soldiers hurry to the governor's and bring him and Mynheer Van Twiller.

And now, reader, we will turn to another part of our story which we left off rather abruptly. We allude to the discovery made by Long Tom and his boat's crew.

As the boat touched the pier, the figure arose and staggered forward a step or two, then fell forward into his arms as he sprang to the side of the boat.

"Saved! saved!" she murmured. "Oh, take me to my home."

"Where is that, ma'am?" asked honest Tom; but he got no answer to his question—she had fainted.

"By thunder, but this is a scrape!" muttered Tom.

"Better shove off, eh?" asked Cam "Sogerman come down here directly and look hard at us!"

"Yes, that's true; shove off into the stream, lads. But what the devil to do with this poor gal is more than I know."

"Why not take her up along with us?" asked one of the crew.

"Got no other choice, I reckon," replied Tom. "Hand us a little of that water from the breaker," he cried to one of the crew, as he raised her head gently. One of the men then handed him a tin cup of water, which he raised carefully to her lips, and managed to force down a few drops.

She sighed, and gave signs of returning consciousness, and now Tom seemed to feel a little more easy.

We will now return to the "Swan" and witness a rather stirring scene there.

When General Clinton and Mynheer Van Twiller received the message of Hans, they at once hurried to the hotel.

"Where is Nicholas Dunderhead?—where is he? Can he tell me where my poor Katrine is?" cried her father, as he rushed into the hotel.

"Ten tousand tollar?" asked Nicholas, very quietly.

"Yes, gladly, so that she is restored to me," replied the father.

"Wall, den, I ton't know for sure were she is, or if der one pe her, put we shall see py and py."

"Be hasty, then, and dare not to trifle with me," cried the father.

"Come along, Mynheer Van Twiller; come along, sheneral—I dink I can find her."

"Lead the prisoner along too," said Sir Henry.

The party started toward the back wing, amid a general murmur of voices and stamping of feet. The noise seemed to have disturbed some of the occupants of the inn, for two doors that lead out on the back piazza were opened and from one room emerged hastily two persons

—from the other two more. The two first the governor recognised as Mr Smith and his brother, who had brought poor Hans to his quarters—the two others, Count Ballentine and his servant.

"What is the matter? What does all this bustle mean?" asked the Count, as he strode forward to the side of Sir Henry.

"Follow us and see—follow us Mr Smith," replied the governor; and then, while several servants came with lights, the entire party hastened to the narrow passage in the back wing, where they stopped at the only door in the passage.

"The key, sir—the key!" cried Sir Henry, pointing to the door, as he turned around sternly to Dorsey.

"Find it yourself—I have no key!" said the detected and now desperate villain.

"Burst the door—this delay is death!" cried a voice from their midst, and the one disguised as Smith sprung forward, followed by his young companion, and both threw themselves against the heavy oaken frame. But they scarcely shook it—it yielded not an inch.

"Go bring a beam—anything to force an entrance!" cried Sir Henry to his attendants.

While they hurried to obey this order, a hurried glance was exchanged between Ricard and Dorsey.

In a moment the servants returned with axes, and soon the door was opened. Then the whole party rushed into the room, but to their astonishment it was unoccupied.

"Villain, where is she?" cried Sir Henry to Dorsey; but the look of the latter was as full of astonishment as his own.

"Aye, tell us where she is, vile wretch! Speak, or I will slay you where you stand," shouted Hunt Ballentine, springing forward and confronting Dorsey.

"Stop, young sir—raise not your hand against your brother!" cried Ricard, in a cold tone of sarcasm.

"My *brother!*—ha, the *rebel!*" echoed Dorsey, now comprehending Ricard's former look.

"Hunt, my son!" groaned the Count, "why are you here?"

"To save her I love, or perish in the attempt!" cried Ballentine.

"Ah, poor, deluded boy, this is a sad hour for thee and thine," sighed the governor. "I have a painful course before me, but it must be followed. You are a prisoner."

"Aye, and that young rebel by his side, Karl Van Twiller, that old man's son, and the brother of the paltry girl you've made so much ado about," cried Dorsey.

"Is this true? serves he with the rebels?" asked the governor of the father.

But Karl stepped forward and answered,—

"I serve America, sir, and I fight for her freedom."

The governor again sighed as he turned to the officer who was with him and said,—

"Let these two young men be guarded. We have no choice but to treat and try them as spies."

The cheek of young Ballentine reddened as he heard this word, and he responded,—

"I came not here, Sir Henry Clinton, as a spy—I came to rescue my betrothed from yon ruthless villain's hands—but now, though I am prisoner, I pray you not to defer searching for her."

"Don't trouble yourself, *brother*," said Dorsey, with a devilish sneer; 'I've no doubt but she's doing well."

"How is this? That Dorsey, surely, is no son of thine?" asked Sir Henry of the Count.

"Ask me not now – anon I will explain all," replied the Count, and hurried from the scene.

"Strange, as it is unfortunate," muttered the governor; then, turning to Dorsey, he asked,—

"Once more, sir, will you say where this old man's daughter is?"

"That's more than I know," responded the villain.

"This mystery must and shall be ferretted out!" cried Sir Henry; then, turning to the unhappy father of Katrine, he added, "remain with me, sir; every nook, den, and house in the city shall undergo a search. If she be alive she shall be found."

CHAPTER XV.

The boat of the "Ocean Queen," with Long Tom and his new-found prize, turned into Helle-gat cove; and as it did so, the lady, who had now recovered as to sit up, gazed at the rocks, and trees, and the house, the outlines of which could be dimly seen in the darkness, and in feeble, but joyful tones, cried,—

"I see my own home before me—this is my father's house."

"Her father's house," muttered Tom. "Why, lady, sure and you must know our skipper? Captain Ballentine's the name he hails by."

"Ballentine—my own Hunt? Yes."

"Bless your starry toplights, why didn't you say so before?"

"I knew you not."

By this time the boat had reached the landing, and Katrine, attended by the honest old coxswain, sprang on shore and hurried to the house.

Here she was only met by a group of terrified attendants, who told her that they knew her father, and Karl, and the captain all must be killed.

"What shall I do?" moaned poor Katrine.

"Blast my eyes if I know!" said old Tom, perfectly at a stand—then an idea seeming to strike him, he added, "If he's got away from 'em alive, he'll make straight for the barkie—if we go aboard we may find him, but if the red-coats have been here it's no use for us to stay."

"Be it as you will—anything to place me by his side if he yet lives—anything but to fall into the hands from which I have but just escaped." And the two returned to the boat.

"I hope it'll blow up fresh, we've little time enough to get clear of the shipping in the narrows afore day breaks," said Tom, as he trimmed his sheets and filled away. "I wish to Moses it would keep dark till noon tomorrow."

Katrine, though relieved from the first and most imminent peril, was now in a miserable state of suspense regarding the fate of her lover. Little did she dream that at the very hour when her boat scudded past the old stone prison which stood upon Whitehall point, that her lover and her brother were both within its walls.

When Dorsey had left Katrine with the terrible threat of returning at ten o'clock, she had, as the reader will remember, grasped the knife, with the intention of taking the life which she thought she could not preserve without dishonour. When she raised the deadly weapon above her quivering bosom, and raised her eyes to take a last glance at the stars which shone down through the single window in her room, one hope, like a ray from one of those stars, seemed to have entered her bosom.

"If I can but reach it I can pass," she said; and she hastened to move an old chest of drawers which stood near, a little closer to the window.

Taking the long silken scarf from her neck, she doubled it round the centre bar, then, grasping the scarf, she lowered herself down to the ground.

Trembling with fear and excitement, she hurried forth from the dark and narrow alley, and rushed down to the end of the pier, falling to the earth exhausted and helpless.

While lying in this miserable state, she saw the white sails of a boat loom up in the darkness beyond her, and uttered the feeble cry which was first heard by honest Tom and his boat's crew.

Sir Henry Clinton, by an artful trick, discovers that Dorsey was really the son of Ricard, who had imposed him upon his unsuspicious master as being the latter's offspring.

Meanwhile Karl and Captain Ballentine were under arrest as spies.

Sir Henry Clinton pitied sincerely his friend Count Ballentine, and also regretted that the captain of the "Ocean Queen" and his lieutenant, Karl, had rushed into the lion's mouth in order to find Katrine.

Sir Henry, therefore, wilfully closed his eyes to a plot which he learned was contemplated to rescue the prisoners.

Ricard and his wife (the mother of Dorsey) had joined Cam and Long Tom in an attempt to free Hunt Ballentine, Karl, and Dorsey from prison.

It needs not to detail all the incidents. Suffice it that the prisoners were apprised of the hour and were ready.

Just as the three prisoners succeeded in lowering themselves by means of a rope thrown up to them by Long Tom, the sentinel saw them and fired. His ball found the heart of Dorsey, who fell mortally wounded.

The others followed Long Tom toward the spot where their boat awaited them.

Down along the pier they rushed. Soon they were by the spile to which the boat was moored. As they sprang in Hunt cried to Tom to shove off, and at the same time seized an oar himself. Karl and Cam followed his example, and in another moment four bending oars were sending the boat out upon the stormy water, quivering as she met the heavy waves which almost hid her in their spray. They had scarcely cleared the end of the pier when the guard were upon it, and ere they were half a musket-shot distant, the officer in command shouted,—

"Stop, you rebels! come back, or I will fire upon you!"

"Stoop low, men!—crouch low in the boat, for they will fire!"

A rattling volley of musketry from the shore told that the officer had kept his threat. A groan from poor Tom was heard; and as the rest raised to their oars, he let go his and then grasped the thwart of the boat, to sustain himself in his seat.

"By heavens, Tom, you are shot!" cried his captain, in a tone of deep anxiety.

"Never mind me, cap'n! See, them are sogers are heaving up signals for the ships below to cut us off! You'd better up sails and get out of this; they'll sarve you worse than they have me."

"By heavens! the noble fellow speaks

true! Karl, take the tiller—Cam, clear away those two lug sails and reef them, quick!"

Hunt then raised the bleeding and gallant old tar, and carried him to the after part of the boat, where he laid him upon his cloak.

"Poor Tom, this is too hard," he groaned. "I must try and bandage your wounds."

"It's no use, cap'n. I've been shot afore, and I knows what it is. I shall only live to see you safe. I know'd it afore I left the ship; for our lady's face was dark and muddy."

"I can explain all. Her eyes are made of looking-glass, slightly coloured—her face is so polished as to reflect colours—therefore, when in blue water they would look blue, in the muddy waters of the harbour they would look like the water!"

"Well, it's no matter, yer honour—it's all over with me now. Raise me up, cap'n—raise me up, and let me take a look round. My eye-sight, like the flame of a taller dip, may be all the brighter afore it goes out! There they are, the bloody sharks, ahead on the starboard bow!—a whole fleet of boats!"

For a moment even his bold heart felt cold, and his cheek grew pale. It was too late to try another course. He had but three men, counting himself, to oppose he knew not how many. But he was not one to despair.

"Keep the boat steady on her course!" said he to Karl; and then he carefully examined the arms which Tom had provided.

It was already evident that the enemy saw them, for the boats were spread out in a line through which they must pass or be taken.

As Tom gazed upon them a singular look of firm determination settled on his pale face.

"Cap'n," said he, "just stuff your handkerchief or something into this hole in my breast to keep the blood in a little longer. I only want to live twenty minutes more!"

Without knowing why Tom wished it, Hunt obeyed his request, and stanched as he best could, the gushing blood, when Tom continued,—

"I mean this, cap'n; you knows, as well as I does, that I can't live an hour, but I'm strong enough to hold that tiller and steer her through amongst them are boats, while you three lay down in the bottom, where they can't hit you. If they carry away the masts, why, then we'll all go together—if they don't you are saved, and it'll be some joy to me to know that when I slip my wind."

Hunt objected. Karl and Cam each volunteered for the dangerous post. But Tom would not be put aside; and he forced them to secure him to the seat by lashings, so that he could not be moved from his perilous post.

Tom steered down with an unwavering hand, heading for a narrow opening between two of the largest boats, and from both of these he was hailed as he came near.

"Heave to, with your boat—heave to!"

Tom made no reply.

"Heave to, you infernal rebels!—heave to, or we'll fire into you!"

Steadily swept on the boat, and Tom spoke not; and now he was directly between the two, while others were pulling rapidly in to intercept him. Again Tom was hailed, again he heard the threat of firing, but as the boat's bow was nearly clear of them and the gale freshened, he laughed out a scornful reply,—

"Fire, you bloody fools! Burn your powder, you can't hurt me!"

"Fire!" cried the enraged officers, and, as his boat got out of range of the others, so that they could fire without doing any harm to their own friends, they opened a terrific volley upon him.

When the smoke cleared away, to their surprise and astonishment the helmsman sat steady and erect as ever; he seemed to have gone untouched through that terrible shower, and now his boat was dashing off at a speed which rendered their pursuit useless, still holding on her course.

But they did not see that the head of poor Tom had dropped upon his breast; they did not know that his whole body was riddled with their balls.

He had got the helm set just to the weather-gage, which it would carry with the sails trimmed as they were; and though his arm was stiff with the ice of death, he never slacked his hold.

The rest of the crew of the boat sprang to their feet after the dreadful line of fire had been passed; but poor Tom spoke no more. He had saved them.

Ere noon on that day, Hunt Ballentine was on his vessel's deck, his betrothed was once more in his arms, and the "Magic Figure-Head" was turned to sea for a cruise, which ended equally as fortunate as any he had previously undertaken.

So it continued until the end of the war, when Captain Ballentine retired with his beautiful Katrine to enjoy the fruits of his love of liberty and independence.

His father, the Count, dying, and entirely reconciled to his son, he left him his vast estates in England.

The Captain, now Count Ballentine, resided on them to the end of his days, except occasionally visiting his brother-in-law, Karl, who had returned to his father, and at the demise of the latter inherited all his wealth, with the exception of a good jointure to Katrine.

Weekly Numbers, One Penny.   Monthly Parts, Sixpence.

The Volume Complete, containing 500 pages and 88 large Illustrations, Price 3/6.

NED KELLY
THE IRONCLAD AUSTRALIAN BUSHRANGER.

The Marvellous and Exciting Career of this Australian Bushranger, whose daring Adventures and Hairbreadth Escapes have, for years past, been the absorbing theme of the Colonial Press, is here minutely recorded. Fiction itself could scarcely surpass in its most extravagant flights, the astounding feats and romantic incidents filling every mouth, in the life of this Land Pirate whose resources, like his courage, seemed to be inexhaustible, and whose daring dexterity paralysed the efforts of the Government, and created a sympathy that almost stifled the horror and indignation created by his Reign of Terror. At considerable cost and trouble, the Editor has been enabled to procure the incidents in the life of this Freebooter from a member of the Melbourne Police, one of the Force by whom Kelly was Hunted down.

LONDON:
Published at the Office, 280, Strand, W.C.

Just Published.   Price Twopence, 64 pp., Crown 8vo.

THE HOME CIRCLE SERIES OF SELECT STORIES,
Written by the most Popular Authors.

These Stories are recommended as suitable for Road, River, or Rail, as also for THE FAMILY CIRCLE.

- No. 1.—Hertha.
- No. 2.—Mary of Moscow.
- No. 3.—Acquitted.
- No. 4.—Little Sweetheart.
- No. 5.—An Iron Grip.
- No. 6.—Weak, but not Wicked.
- No. 7.—Gay Blount; or, Her Fortune.
- No. 8.—A Woman Scorned.
- No. 9.—Beauty's Battle.
- No. 10.—A Noble Woman.
- No. 11.—Countess's Crime.
- No. 12.—Near Relations.

LONDON:
Published at the Office, 280, Strand, W.C.

THE GREAT MEDICINE.

Effervescing and Tasteless, forms a most Refreshing Beverage. Gives instant relief in Headache, Sea or Bilious Sickness, Constipation, Indigestion, Lassitude, Heartburn & Feverish Colds; prevents and quickly cures the worst form of Typhus, Scarlet and other Fevers, Smallpox, Measles, and Eruptive or Skin Complaints, and various other altered conditions of the blood.

The Testimony of MEDICAL GENTLEMEN, *and the Professional Press has been unqualified in praise of*

LAMPLOUGH'S PYRETIC SALINE

as possessing most important elements calculated to restore and maintain health, with perfect vigour of body and mind.

"Have it in your houses, and forget it not in your travels."

Dr. Prout.—"Unfolding germs of immense benefit to mankind."

Dr. Morgan.—"It furnishes the blood with its lost saline constituents."

Dr. Turley.—"I found it act as a specific in my experience and family in the *worst form of Scarlet Fever*, no other medicine being required."

Dr. S. Gibbon (formerly Physician of the London Hospital.— "Its usefulness in the treatment of disease has long been confirmed by medical experience. I have been in the habit of using it in private practice for many years."

Dr. Sparks (Government Medical Inspector of Emigrants from the Port of London) writes: "I have great pleasure in bearing my cordial testimony to its efficacy in the treatment of many of the ordinary and chronic forms of GASTRIC COMPLAINTS and other forms of FEBRILE DYSPEPSIA."

In Bottles, 2s 6d., 4s. 6d., 11s., and 21s. each.

Dr. Powel's Balsamic Lozenges,

For Coughs, Asthmatic, Bronchial, and Consumptive Complaints.

These excellent Lozenges, prepared only by H. LAMPLOUGH, have for many years been found of great service; their occasional use often prevents attacks from colds and inflammation. Price 1s. 1½d. per Box.

May be obtained of all Chemists, and of the Proprietor.

H. LAMPLOUGH, 113, Holborn, London, E.C.

www.ingramcontent.com/pod-product-compliance
Lightning Source LLC
Chambersburg PA
CBHW032229230426
43666CB00033B/1650